THREE CHEERS FOR THE
NEXT MAN TO DIE

THREE CHEERS FOR THE NEXT MAN TO DIE

Dudley Anderson

21·01·16

ISIS
LARGE PRINT
Oxford

Copyright © Dudley Anderson, 1983

First published in Great Britain 1983
by Robert Hale Limited

Published in Large Print 2003 by ISIS Publishing Ltd,
7 Centremead, Osney Mead, Oxford OX2 0ES
by arrangement with Robert Hale Limited

British Library Cataloguing in Publication Data
Anderson, Dudley
  Three cheers for the next man to die –
  Large print ed. –
  (Isis reminiscence series)
  1. Anderson, Dudley
  2. Great Britain. Army. Devonshire Regiment.
  Battalion, 12th – History
  3. World War, 1939–1945 – Personal narratives, British
  4. World War, 1939–1945 – Campaigns
  5. Large type books
  I Title
  940.5'41241'092

ISBN 0–7531–9788–X (hb)
ISBN 0–7531–9789–8 (pb)

Printed and bound by Antony Rowe, Chippenham

This book is dedicated to the boys of
'D' Company who didn't come back

Contents

Preface

This book is not intended to be a history of the Red Devons, the 12th battalion of the Devonshire Regiment who were in the 6th Air Landing Brigade of the 6th Airborne Division.

It is a book that I have written as a vocational exercise during a period of inactivity from my career brought about by illness. Following the crash in the property world in the mid-1970s I suffered two heart attacks, the aftermath of which caused me to change my lifestyle.

This is the first book I have ever written or tried to write and I would like to thank all my friends and family who helped and gave me encouragement, my Secretary who typed the first manuscript several times, and Lt.-Colonel James Langley OBE MC, author of *To Fight Another Day*, who edited my book for me and hopefully showed me what writing was about.

When I was demobilised from the Army in 1947 I could not get back into civilian life quick enough. I wanted nothing more to do with the Army. Looking back now, I realize it was an experience that I would not want to have missed, and I think that the lives of

1

the young people of today would be enhanced if National Service were still in existence. It would help them to fend for themselves and give them employment, training, discipline, comradeship and adventure.

I served with the Red Devons during the Second World War and took part in their three major operations, the Normandy Landings, the Ardennes and the Rhine Crossing, and ever since the war I had thought that one day I would like to express my feelings in writing about going into military action.

In the years since the war I have met many men who served in the Armed Forces during that period, and it seemed to me that for each man in the front line there must have been hundreds backing him up because none of these men had ever taken part in a bayonet charge while I was in two. Nevertheless the first thing people ask is "What was it like? How did you feel?"

Therefore what I want my readers to understand, and perhaps even live through me, is what the war was like for a nineteen-year-old youth at the sharp end of a military operation as opposed to the majority of views expressed in war books that have been written by informed commentators or high-ranking officers of the various services. I am sure that the feelings I experienced were similar to those of the assault troops during the recent Falkland Islands campaign — but they were professionals and we were conscripted amateurs.

In the nearly forty years that have ensued since the Second World War my memory of incidents and exploits has naturally grown dim; I must confess, therefore, that while some of my accounts are as true as I can remember, others are based on the rumours and counter-rumours ever present at the battle front, while still others are pure fiction. I would also like to state quite emphatically that none of the characters of any rank or command in this book portrays or is intended to portray men of the Red Devons, living or dead, with whom I served. I sincerely hope that if any of my former comrades-in-arms or their families read this book they will not be offended but will relive their own experiences with pleasure and pride.

What I have contrived to convey, and I am confident I have done so accurately, is the backcloth under which we served together with the fog of war, the fear, the uncertainty and the comradeship in the life of a young soldier who was in action at "Slit-Trench Level".

Dudley Anderson

CHAPTER ONE

The Battle of Breville

The silence of the pitch-black cavern which was the hold of the LST (Landing Ship Tank) was broken by a Welsh baritone voice singing the chorus of the song of the 6th Airborne Division, to the tune of "The Red River Valley":

> So come stand by the bar with your glasses,
> Drink a toast of the men of the sky,
> Drink a toast to the men dead already,
> THREE CHEERS FOR THE NEXT MAN
>   TO DIE.

At first a solo performance, the song swelled in volume as one and then another voice joined in. By the last line every one of the hundreds of Red Devils lying and sitting in the hold of the ship were singing as loudly and enthusiastically as their wounds would allow.

THREE CHEERS FOR THE
NEXT MAN TO DIE.

We had all been in the assault on Normandy — the Second Front — which had begun on 6th June — D-Day — 1944 and had been wounded in action in the battles for the bridgehead. Now we were amongst the first casualties to be shipped back to hospital in England. By no means out of danger, we had been shaken by several near misses from bombs which had damaged the ship, putting out all the lights in our over-crowded hold.

The ship pitched and rolled not only to the normal Channel swell but also to the waves created by the bombing. Strapped helplessly to a stretcher and anyway immobile by reason of my wounded leg, I sang as loudly as the rest. As a boy of nineteen it was the only way I knew to keep my spirits up and my mind off what would happen if the Jerry planes were a little luckier.

The last thirty-six hours had been so far the most momentous of my life.

That battered village of Breville had etched itself on my memory. After being driven out, the Germans had won it back, crashing in at first light with tanks. If they could have pushed on beyond the village and captured the two vital bridges over the river and the canal, they could turn the Allied flank and roll our troops back into a narrowing bridgehead.

The 51st Highlanders were brought up. They tried an assault on the village and failed. They tried again and once more were thrown back. So, late in the afternoon of 12th June, we who were the last reserves of the 6th Airborne Division, the Red Devils, were lined up for yet another attack. D Company, mine, was to lead it. We were dropping with weariness, but so too were the Germans, and like us they had had their force badly depleted by casualties.

Crouching under a hedge, I watched the barrage that preceded our advance, bouncing along the road a hundred yards in front of us into Breville. It was effective: the Germans retired. But as we left our meagre shelter, the German mortars started a counter barrage. We dodged along the streets with the bombs hitting the walls and roofs above our heads. It was then that I saw my platoon commander, Lieutenant "Flannelfoot" Guthrie, killed. He was blown halfway across the road and lay crumpled, like an old sack, against the corner of a cottage. The village wallowed in smoke, fires blazed everywhere, and the guns of both sides competed to see which could contribute most to the hellish din.

Well, we were in Breville, but for how long? Most of our troops and some commandos occupied a large church and other buildings in the centre of the village, while D Company was ordered to defend the outskirts.

On the east of the village was an orchard. Among the trees we lined up two platoons strong, with our eyes on the Germans who, a hundred yards away, were preparing a counter-attack. Our bayonets were already fixed, so we charged first.

I was nearly at the left end of the line. Joe French, the Bren-gunner, and my friend Bill Simpson were beyond me with the rest of the platoon on my right. As I rushed forward gripping my rifle, I found myself screaming and yelling like we did when we were kids playing cowboys and Indians. So were all the others, although I could hardly hear them. The mad cacophony of the guns and mortars submerged all other sounds; we were being drowned by noise. The training and discipline of the past months drove us on, even though men were dropping all around. Some were victims of German machine-guns or mortar bombs, but some alas of our own barrage which was beginning to fall short.

A mortar bomb exploded between Joe and myself, and we half dived, half hurtled to the ground. It was a curious sensation. I felt no particular pain, yet I knew something had happened, I sensed that I had been hit.

Lying on the ground, Joe and I continued firing at the enemy no more than seventy yards away. Glancing back for a moment, I saw that everyone was on the ground except our Company Commander, Major John Barnfield, who was running up and down the line like a man demented and shouting at the top of his voice, "This is our shining hour." It sounds trite, but for him it was typical. He had discarded his steel helmet and was wearing his red beret, the badge that every Red Devil wears with pride. Then a shell splinter carried off the top of his head.

Sergeant Walters, in command of our platoon now that Lieutenant Guthrie was dead, dashed across to see if he could do anything to help. He was within five yards of the major when the front of his flying-smock was suddenly stitched across as though with red thread by machine-gun bullets. He died instantly. Nobody could stand up in that holocaust for long, and live.

Then we became aware of a slight lessening in the barrage. Easing ourselves onto hands and knees, Joe and I scuttled back some thirty or forty yards to where the first house of Breville loomed above the splintered and smoking trees. We dived into a slit trench, only to find three commandos already lying in the bottom. We wriggled down, glad of the cover, and then more men arrived — until there were eight of us in all — the uppermost protruding above ground level.

I ran my hand over my leg, my thigh, my groin. There was a numbness, and my fingers were covered with blood. I have never been able to understand how I was able to run forty yards with a six-inch wound in my groin and another in my thigh. But while I lay in the trench I knew only that I had been wounded, to what extent I had no idea. If I had died then, I could not have cared less about the three cheers. I would have just slipped into unconsciousness without even much discomfort.

Joe had been wounded by the same mortar bomb and had collected three further wounds in his back as he was making for the slit trench. The pressure was now lifted as the second wave of troops passed over us to the attack, joined by the twenty or thirty men from D Company who had survived unhurt. Lying there, I watched them — mostly paratroopers and commandos, with Bill Simpson running with them and yelling like a fiend as they charged across the orchard. The barrage had stopped, and the German mortars had been silenced, so it was hand-to-hand fighting. Half a dozen fanatical Germans jumped out of their trenches and started running towards us with their bayonets at the ready, but they went down quickly before our charge. I saw Bill stab a German in the middle of his body, withdraw his bayonet and charge on just as if he was going round the assault course on Salisbury Plain.

Soon the remaining Germans in their slit trenches were surrendering at bayonet point. There was nothing else for them to do. Like us they had fought for a week almost without respite; they had withstood a terrible artillery battering and were tired, dishevelled and beaten.

Sprawled in my slit trench, I saw a paratroop major ordering his own men back to their own lines, escorting prisoners. Bill Simpson and Eddie Faulkner, another D Company man, were with them and were detailed to take three SS troopers including an officer back to Brigade HQ for interrogation. I saw Bill and Eddie take away their prisoners' weapons, including the officer's Schmeisser submachine carbine, and search them for other weapons. They were not thorough enough. As they were marching across the orchard in the gloom, dodging in and out amongst the trees, one of the Germans suddenly pulled out a concealed dagger. With a quick upward thrust in the small of the back, just as we had been taught to strike, he pierced Bill Simpson's heart, killing him instantly. Eddie shot the man at once. Then, as the other two looked as though they were about to run away, he shot them both in a blind fury. Almost immediately he broke down, crying, and had to be helped back to our lines.

I felt like crying too. I could not blame Eddie, nor could anyone else, for letting the stern mask of a Red Devil slip for a moment. It was a terrible thing to have happened to two young lads. But we had all learned a lesson. Never again were any members of D Company caught out through slack searching of a prisoner.

As the fighting died down, I eased myself out of the trench and sat on the edge. Even in the restricted range of vision possible through the eddying smoke, I could see literally dozens of bodies in heaps under the trees. Most were motionless and evidently dead, but others wriggled and jerked spasmodically. Some groaned and called for help.

Joe French had disappeared. Afterwards I learned that, despite five shrapnel wounds, he was still able to walk somehow and so had managed to struggle unaided back to the first-aid post. I thought I would try to do the same, but as soon as I tried to stand, I knew that it was impossible. I just had to sit there until help came.

Sergeant-Major Bill Maynard appeared through the murk shouting for stretcher-bearers. Presently I could see a few first-aid men moving about, but they must have been outnumbered about ten to one by the casualties. I was lucky. I spotted a couple of first-aid men I knew well, Arthur and Harold Newing, who were twin brothers from Plymouth. Having been left in reserve, they had now been drafted in to lend a hand to the stretcher-bearers. They were good chaps, though not the best soldiers in the Company. They sang well, played the banjo and, in happier days of training in England, had been much in demand for camp entertainments. However, it seemed that first aid was one subject for which they did not have a natural aptitude. Despite the fact that all we Red Devils were supposed to have intensive first-aid training, they stood there, nonplussed. I had to take charge.

"Come on, Harold," I yelled. "For Christ's sake get weaving and get me out of here before the jerries come back."

I pulled down my trousers as far as I could, pointed out the great wound in my groin and suggested he got busy with his field dressing. Harold went white and looked away as he fumbled for his dressing. The one he produced was far too small, so I shouted to him (I was feeling faint by this time and my voice sounded far away) to find a bigger one. I knew he had one as they had been issued to us just before D-Day, and mine was in ribbons where the shrapnel had hit me. "Sorry," said Harold. This time he had more success. He made quite a reasonable job of tying the dressing and even avoided cutting my battledress too much.

While all this was going on, the sounds of battle were no further away than the end of the orchard, and I began to feel apprehensive. Lying there, virtually helpless and without rifle or ammunition, I was poorly placed if the Germans managed to put in a counter-attack. Also my leg was starting to hurt. The numbness was fading. I found the leg was bent back but dared not try straightening it, for fear of doing further damage.

"For God's sake, hurry up and get me back to the first-aid post," I yelled.

The Newings looked around for a stretcher, but none was to be found. So, with one arm draped round each of their shoulders. I hoisted myself up and, using my good left leg as a kind of crutch, staggered out of the orchard. Not far away was a first-aid post set up in a farmyard, where we were lucky enough to find a stretcher. The Newings laid me on it to wait for treatment, and as they went back to the orchard to rescue more wounded, I called my thanks.

CHAPTER TWO

Homeward Bound

Then the shelling started again, and the first-aid post became a fair replica of hell. The farmhouse, barns and the farmyard itself were packed to overflowing, with more wounded arriving every minute. Our second in command, Captain "Pongo" Trelawney, came in on a stretcher with half a leg missing but still wearing his red beret. As he passed me, he sat up, shook his fist towards the German lines and shouted, "They got me, the bastards, but I'll be back." I do not know whether he ever did, but he had the right spirit.

Somebody started giving orders to get the wounded farther back. No ambulances were available, but those maids-of-all-work the jeeps had been fitted out to carry six stretcher cases — two across the bonnet, two on the back and two strapped to the roof. Three of them crept into the farmyard and started loading up, but as these were all that could be mustered, it was going to take a very long time to evacuate all of us wounded.

Then I had a stroke of luck. I spotted Pat Tomkins of D Company. Pat was an older man than most of us, thirty if he was a day. He was married with a couple of kids and had refused chances of promotion because he liked being a private. A real cockney, he was a born scrounger and was highly thought of by our Company Commander because of his skill in procuring an adequate supply of booze and other essentials for the Company Officers' mess. What was more to the point, he drove the Company Commander's jeep and was doing so now.

Pat was doing good work, evacuating wounded under fire — naturally those nearest to hand, but when he saw me, he was not averse to showing a bit of preference. Five minutes were all that were necessary to strap my stretcher to the back of the jeep, and away we went. We had, as a matter of fact, a load of eight casualties, for two walking wounded were sitting beside Pat. Through the bursting shells, out of the inferno of the farmyard and down dark lanes lit only by star shells and parachute flares, our overloaded jeep jolted along to the casualty clearing station. This turned out to be a rambling old mansion with a Red Cross draped across its entire front. By this time, as it was nearly dark, the Germans were unable to see it, and the house and grounds were being shelled and bombed, but not with such intensity as the farmyard.

Unloading only took a few minutes. We were dumped on the ground outside the house and left lying there, waiting for medical orderlies to carry us into the building for treatment. But again there were insufficient staff to deal with the wounded, and men on stretchers were lying all around. Pat was reluctant to leave me there with the rest, but he had no choice. The best he could do was to find me a little shelter from the bombardment by getting the stretcher-bearers to lay me in the shadow of the great stone staircase that led up to the front door. The stairs certainly gave me some sort of protection. Unfortunately I was so much in the shadow that I was continually being overlooked by the medical orderlies.

I do not know how long I was lying there. At least an hour, maybe two, but for some of the time I was hardly conscious. Presently, it must have been well after midnight, a despatch rider rode up and happened to prop his motor-bike alongside my stretcher.

"Hullo, what are you doing here?" he asked. I told him. "Never mind, old son," he said cheerfully, "I'll soon get you inside."

At that moment a German plane came zooming over, its machine-guns firing. I could see the tracers coming towards us. With no hesitation, the DR threw himself on top of me, completely shielding my body until the danger was past. Then he got up and went for a medical orderly. Together they carried me up the stairs and into the main hall, where they placed my stretcher on the floor. Then, before I could even say thank you or cheerio, the despatch rider was gone. I never saw him again.

The discomfort of being moved into the building brought me back to full consciousness. Now followed another interminable period of waiting which gave me ample time to study my surroundings, though somewhat distracted by the increasing pain in my groin. Lying on my back on the stretcher, I examined the ceiling, which was a very fine one, as I could appreciate from my early upbringing in a builder's family. It was splendidly decorated with plaster mouldings, and from it hung several ornate crystal chandeliers. The walls of the vast hall were panelled in hardwood, and a magnificent oak staircase led up to a gallery. The place had obviously been the home of someone of wealth and importance.

The Army had predictably introduced an element of pure utility. Nailed to the panelling over every door and window were Army blankets, groundsheets, tarpaulins and anything to prevent light showing outside. A petrol-driven generator that I could hear puttering away somewhere in the background provided electricity for the rather feeble lights which were roughly fixed to the walls.

At least a hundred stretcher cases were crammed into the hall, but only three medical orderlies were moving about among them. From what I could see, their task was to sort out the living from the dead and administer pain-killing injections to those who needed them. After a while one of the orderlies came across and asked if I was in pain. He was a fair-haired lad, no older than myself, and the blood on his white overalls made him look like a novice butcher. When I nodded, he cut away a piece of my trousers and jabbed a syringe in my behind saying with a smile, "Why can't you Airborne blokes keep yourselves out of trouble?" Then he was walking through the ranks of wounded and calling, "Anyone still in pain? Anyone want more morphia?" Young though he was, he was doing a man's work that night.

The realization that I had been wounded and the possible implications had come to me very gradually, but now I began to worry. Did I have internal injuries? Would I lose my leg? Was I going to die? The anxieties were spinning round and round in my mind when, helped by the morphia, I relapsed into unconsciousness.

I dimly remember being loaded into an ambulance just as dawn was breaking, and thinking that it was more comfortable than the jeep. Then I was being unloaded at a tented field hospital near one of the beaches. I could hear the waves breaking, as they had on the shores of Anglesey when I was a boy, only those few short years ago. I fell asleep again.

The Army doctor came to dress my wound at around eight o'clock in the morning, which I worked out was exactly twelve hours after I had been hit. When he took off the field dressing, he said, "You're lucky." He pointed out that no major blood vessels had been pierced and that, if the wound had been half an inch higher or half an inch to the left, the splinter would have penetrated my abdomen and killed me. So I suppose I had had some luck, if you can call being wounded at all lucky.

More injections. Tetanus and other drugs this time, as well as morphia. My backside was beginning to feel like a pincushion. "Back to England with you, my lad," said the doctor. That sounded good news. I started to doze off again, then roused myself for a moment as I remembered a piece of advice from my training days. What was it they said RAMC stood for? "Rob all my comrades." No doubt a shocking libel on a body of worthy men, but nevertheless I felt around making sure all my personal belongings were still there — my watch, my money, my papers.

The next time I became conscious, I was being carried from the tent and loaded into a DUKW — pronounced "duck" and named after its maker's code: D for year of origin, U for utility, K for front-wheel drive and W for six wheeled. An amphibious vehicle which carried about a dozen stretchers, it weighed 14,000 pounds and had a capacity of 25 troops or 5,000 pounds of cargo. Its maximum speed on land was 50 m.p.h. and 5.5 knots on water. When it was full, we careered off over an open field and down to the beach where, exactly seven days earlier, D Company had scrambled ashore through the surf. The weather had not changed much. The sky was overcast and the sea still choppy. The DUKW charged down the beach and made for an LST lying about half a mile offshore.

These LSTs were largish boats, quite capable of an ocean passage, and equipped with two massive doors opening onto a steep ramp which led into the hold in which tanks were normally carried. Now that their primary task had been accomplished, they were moored there waiting to evacuate the wounded.

Once we were through the surf, we found ourselves in a swell, the aftermath of a storm, with waves about six feet high. It was a rougher sea than the DUKW had been designed for, and we bobbed about like a cork. It was just as well that we were strapped to our stretchers and that the stretchers were fastened to convenient points in the hold.

There were at least a dozen LSTs grouped fairly close together, and at last our driver arrived at one of them. Now to get us aboard. It was like trying to thread a needle while standing on a cake-walk. We had to get into position, wait for a wave to lift us up and carry us towards the top of the ramp leading into the ship, and then make our entry before the receding waves dropped us back.

We failed to make it. About six feet from the top of the ramp the wheels lost their traction and started to spin. Another wave carried the ship away from us and, although our wheels were revving at full speed, we were slowly slipping backwards. Within a minute we were wallowing in the sea again and assessing our slim chances of survival if the DUKW capsized.

"What are you chaps worrying about back there?" called out the driver, divining our thoughts. "We're OK." We were glad he thought so.

"Get out of the way!" yelled another DUKW driver, who had better luck than we did, for he got his vehicle on board first time. We had to back away and make a complete circuit before we could gain a place in the queue.

Joking and swearing, our driver made four more unsuccessful attempts to get the DUKW into the ship. "One more go," announced that harassed man, "and if we don't do it this time, we'll have to go back and load you onto another DUKW. I'm burning the clutch out of this one."

We charged in at maximum speed on a surging wave and got to within a few feet of the top of the ramp. Then back we started to slither again, but not for long. Our slide back into the sea was arrested by a bump. Another DUKW, which had discharged its own cargo of wounded and spotted our predicament, had come up behind us and parked itself solidly on the ramp. Then it gave us a push upwards, and with the two engines pushing we eventually climbed over the hump and slid gratefully into the hold of the LST.

Compared to the DUKW, the interior of the LST looked positively huge. I felt as Jonah must have on finding himself inside the whale. No sooner had the DUKW come to a halt than sailors started unloading the stretchers, which they parked in three tiers on bunks along the sides of the ship. The walking wounded sat on the deck or strolled about.

We hung about, waiting, on the heaving sea until nightfall. It was a wearisome business, but the Navy made it lighter by sharing out some cigarettes and rum with us. They were welcome. So were the rounds of a medical officer and his hypodermic syringe, even though the needles seemed to be getting blunter every time I felt them.

I dozed, and when I woke up, it was the middle of the night and the convoy was the target for an aerial attack. There came an alarming crash and explosion, as a stick of bombs landed in the sea alongside. The ship heeled over at a frightening angle, the lights fused and the singing started.

So come stand by the bar with your glasses,
Drink a toast to the men of the sky,
Drink a toast to the men dead already,
THREE CHEERS FOR THE NEXT MAN
    TO DIE.

At the moment that seemed likely to be all of us, but somehow that did not seem so bad with us all singing. In the intervals, though, I prayed hard and then fell asleep and did not wake up until we pulled in to Portsmouth Harbour.

The sun was shining as we were carried ashore to the cheers of a group of dockyard workers. We were taken direct to a hospital train for transfer somewhere or another; we did not know where. During all this movement some kindly ladies from a voluntary organization came along, giving out cards with the inscription: "I have been wounded. I am back in England." They asked for the names and addresses of our next-of-kin and sent the cards off for us. It was a much-appreciated service, especially in my case, for my mother received it by the same post as a letter she had sent to me which was returned with "Missing, presumed killed" stamped on the envelope.

CHAPTER
THREE

"The Volunteers"

The last time I had seen my family was about a year earlier. I said goodbye to them when I joined the Airborne Division. And the first time I heard that Airborne song, "Three cheers for the next man to die", was in the summer of 1943, in the Stonehenge Inn on Salisbury Plain.

That evening we were a group of youngsters, all eighteen or nineteen, freshly attired in Army battledress and wearing the red beret, the headgear of the Airborne Forces. On the upper sleeve of our tunics was stitched the symbol of Bellerophon, bearing a spear and riding on the winged horse Pegasus. Although we did not know it, we were to achieve fame as the Sixth Airborne Division, which spearheaded some of the major advances across northern Europe from the Normandy Invasion until VE-Day found it deep in the heart of Germany. We were all technically volunteers, but, as will be seen, some of us were more voluntary than others. The emphasis is on the word "technically".

I was eighteen in December 1942, registered for National Service in January, had my medical examination in February and was called up by the Army in March 1943.

With my calling-up papers I received a railway warrant to travel to the little mining town of Ossett in Yorkshire. I was told to report for duty at the General Service Corps depot on 18th March, bringing with me only a minimum amount of personal belongings including my National Identity Card and my ration book. On the train from Norfolk, which was then my home, I met several other lads of the same age, all bound for Ossett and all very apprehensive about what lay ahead. For most of them it was their first experience of having to fend for themselves, away from home, but not for me.

Suffolk was my native county, but in the mid-1930s the family moved to London, where my father found work with a builder, but as the war became imminent, he worked as a builder's foreman on airfields and army camps which were springing up all over the country, and we only saw him at weekends. I was one of four children, with an older sister and a younger brother and sister, so as the "man of the family" when my father was away, I had to carry responsibility at an earlier age than most boys.

Initially we lived in the East End of London, but during the blitz in the autumn of 1940 we moved to North Wales where my father had been lucky enough to rent a furnished farm-house. Almost immediately I got a job, my first, since there was no question of my going back to school. My school in the East End had been evacuated to some distant country place before the summer holidays, and no one had time to bother about a stray like me. So my father took me along to the company offices and without hesitation I was taken on as an office boy in the surveyor's department. This seemed natural enough to me, as not only had my father always been in the building trade but so also had my grandfather and several of my uncles.

We lived happily in Anglesey for about a year until my father had to move on, first to York and then to Norfolk, where he found another house to rent and the family joined him. This time I did not go with them as I liked my job and I liked living in Anglesey, so I stayed on in lodgings and did not live at home again until just before my call-up.

I therefore had the advantage of having to fend for myself for the best part of two years, and I guessed the experience would serve me well in the Army. I felt sorry for some of the other lads, who were decidedly jittery, but I felt I could look after myself and made a resolution that no one was going to take advantage of me.

As the train pulled in to the station, we recruits alighted and were mustered into groups of about thirty, which we soon learned were called squads or platoons.

In charge of us was a big, broad, raw-boned Yorkshireman called Sergeant Grimshaw, a regular peace-time soldier and a veteran of Dunkirk. We could not have held him more in awe if he had been a five-star general, and his opening remarks laid the pattern for the next six weeks.

"I'm going to make soldiers out of you, you showers, whether you like it or not," he yelled. "You may have broken your mothers' hearts, but you won't break mine."

Then he ordered us to produce our civilian ration books and tore out all the sweet, tinned food and clothing coupons with the comment, "You won't be needing these any more." However, he was unlucky with me as I had given my mother all mine, and I earned a black look and some sarcastic comments.

The rest of the day was spent in documentation, fitting out with uniforms, medical inspection, which included vaccination and inoculation, and finally parcelling up our civilian clothes and sending them home. This seemed to cut the last link with family life. We were soldiers now.

I doubt whether we looked like it as, during the next thirty-six hours while we recovered from our injections, we marched up to the cookhouse three times a day — that is, if we felt like eating. Having received no drill training at all, we must have looked a real shambles, more so since we were inclined to regard ourselves as already war casualties.

The thirty-six-hour respite over, we settled down to six weeks of Army drill and aptitude tests. There was plenty of hustling and bullying on the parade ground, but it was surprising how quickly we got used to it, and I realized, for the first time, how resilient human beings are and how quickly they can get used to almost anything.

The officers and NCOs of the General Service Corps who carried out the aptitude tests were quite a reasonable lot and tried to make life at least bearable for us newcomers. They must have found their job frustrating in the extreme, though I daresay they had a good laugh in the Mess over some of our mishaps. Whether any notice was taken over the marking of the tests is a matter for some doubt, as in our squad every man with an A1 medical grade found himself automatically sent to an infantry training centre at Colchester.

During the six weeks I made two particular friends, the first "Tiger" Charlesworth, who was a mild-mannered lad, rather scholastic and unlikely to make much of a soldier. He leaned on the other two of us quite a lot, but we did not mind. His Christian name was Frank, but as we already had one Frank in the squad he was dubbed, with typical adolescent humour, "Tiger". The other Frank, Frank Bailey, was the exact antithesis of "Tiger". He was tall, fair, good-looking, a fine athlete and obviously splendid material for a soldier. Unfortunately he refused to accept Army discipline and spent much of his time on jankers, that is confined to barracks doing such menial tasks as cleaning out latrines and peeling potatoes. For more serious offences there was the "glasshouse" or military prison. Frank was the first soldier the glasshouse staff at Colchester could remember who actually served time during his first three months in the army! Together we formed a closely knit, self-sufficient group. Frank had all the dash, but I think I contributed the caution and

27

cunning, while Tiger just tagged along and did what he was told.

Colchester was a garrison town in Roman times, and the barracks seemed antiquated enough to have survived from that era. They consisted of three old-fashioned two-storey blocks with a high prison-type wall along the fourth side, surrounding the barrack square, and not a tree or blade of grass was in sight. It was a real brick and concrete jungle, where the predators who prowled through it were sergeant-majors and drill sergeants, seeking luckless young recruits as their prey.

Life was much tougher than at Ossett, and I soon decided that the main task of the training staff was to make life as miserable as possible for us, with endless parades and inspections, a roll-call twice a day, marching drill and, worst of all, church parades every Sunday, when we were inspected no less than three times — it was enough to put you off religion. Still all this drove us closer together for comradeship, and certainly we learned how to keep going under extreme provocation.

After fourteen weeks we heard with some excitement that we were to be posted to an infantry battalion; it could not, we thought be worse than the infantry training centre.

Our first shock on arriving at our new station was to discover that we had been drafted to an Airborne Division. Britain had only two such divisions at that time, and both were building up to operational strength. We were to contribute by helping to form a battalion of the Sixth Air Landing Brigade which would have the distinction of flying into battle in gliders. All Airborne troops were volunteers, receiving additional pay as danger money, and we three were therefore very surprised to find ourselves drafted! However, a tough-looking sergeant-major made all technically correct at our first parade when he barked out in his most intimidatory manner that he understood that we had all volunteered but that, if anyone had not done so, he had only to take two paces forward. He stopped shouting and glared at us. Needless to say, nobody moved. So now we were all volunteers, but that is how it happened that some were more voluntary than others.

A brief explanation of the organization of the Airborne Divisions is desirable at this stage since the traditional formation of infantry divisions in the Army had to be adapted to suit the carrying-capacity of aircraft and gliders.

A glider battalion consisted of four companies in addition to specialist troops at headquarters. Each company had four platoons, each of thirty men, since this was the seating-capacity of the Horsa glider, the standard British glider for carrying troops into action. The battalion into which we were drafted already had three companies — A, B and C. We were to form D Company.

Most of the men in the existing companies were conscripts who had volunteered, but there was also a smattering of old soldiers from the pre-war regular army. For our new D Company the senior officers and NCOs were transferred in, not altogether willingly we gathered, from the established Companies. Apart from these, our new Company was entirely of young conscripts, not one of whom, in the four platoons, had reached his nineteenth birthday. D Company was familiarly known as "Dog Company", and it is no wonder that the men of the other companies referred to us as the "the puppy dogs". All we "puppy dogs" had had similar Army experience to date, but now we were Red Devils — at least on paper. And to underline the fact, on pay parade we pocketed an extra shilling a day as danger money. We soon found we were to earn it!

At our first parade we were addressed by our new Company Commander, Major John Barnfield, a tall, good-looking man in his late thirties. We found him very firm but very fair, and he soon became a father figure to most of us. He was a fanatic about sport, with an ambition to see D Company surpass the other companies in every activity, and we soon realized that it paid us to be good at sports as well as being good soldiers.

"You are now Red Devils," he said, "members of a *corps d'élite*. You are second best to no one. You are going to be better than the Guards on the drill square, more mobile than the Armoured and Motorized Division on the battlefield, and more resourceful and tenacious than the commandos in tight situations. You will become highly skilled in the use of all weapons, both Allied and enemy, and, above all, you will become the fittest troops of any Army in the world."

He certainly made an impression, and a year later we were all convinced of the truth of his words.

CHAPTER
FOUR

Weapon Training

Company Sergeant-Major Bill Maynard now took us in hand and proceeded to do his best to weld us into this magnificent fighting force the major had talked about. He had an uphill task. Everyone knew that we were preparing for D-Day, but nobody had the slightest idea when it would be, and according to our NCOs, if we had to wait till Doomsday, we would hardly be ready for it.

Right from the start of training, things went wrong. They were only small things at first, but within the first two or three days several of us were placed on charges and confined to barracks. As for the rest, whenever we wanted to go to the local pub or the pictures of an evening, we had to report for inspection and, since we were never considered smart enough, we were never allowed out. No matter how hard we tried, all we met with was criticism. "You're not good enough yet," snarled the sergeant-major. "Back to your kennels." The platoon sergeants of course backed up the CSM, and as at this time there were no junior officers available to act as platoon commanders, we had no one other than the major to whom we could take our grievances. At this stage of our Army career we were far too much in awe of him to consider approaching him direct, so discontent festered and grew. Something had to break.

One evening when we wanted to go out, we made a special effort to make our huts extra tidy and were all dressed to kill when into the hut came Platoon Sergeant Walters. "What a bloody mess," he yelled. "This place is filthy!" And he decreed that we should stay in and spend the evening cleaning it up. It was the last straw.

"We'll show him what a bloody mess is," we vowed, and we did. Kit was tossed all over the floor, beds were turned upside down and the walls were sprayed with water.

We felt sorry that it was Sergeant Walters we were baiting, for he was quite a decent chap, and later we developed a great respect, even fondness, for him since he was efficient without making a lot of fuss. However, in these early days he was obviously having to do as the CSM told him, whether he approved or not. When he returned to the hut an hour later, he was completely flabbergasted but quickly realized he had a mutiny on his hands which he decided he did not want to handle himself, so he sent off for the CSM.

While we were waiting, several of us rushed off to the other huts for support, and by the time the CSM arrived he was faced with a deputation from the whole company. He now had to decide whether to call in the major and the military police or to try to cope with the situation single-handed. The fact that he chose the latter course convinced us that, in refusing us privileges, he had been acting on his own initiative and would not want the major to know what he had been up to. He now gave us a pep talk, saying that he was driving us hard for our own benefit and survival and pointing out the dangers in going into action untrained and unprepared. For the first time he told us he was satisfied with the way we were shaping, but he added that we still had a hell of a long way to go.

"Now, lads," he said, "don't you think you are better soldiers than when you first arrived here?"

We admitted we were.

It was obviously time for a reappraisal by all, continued the CSM, adding that he admired the spirit that had developed, but this spirit must be harnessed for actions other than mutiny. He concluded by saying that, since the first phase of our initiation into the Airborne was complete, he was prepared to overlook this incident and, when the hut was cleaned up, we could go out for the evening, but woe betide us if it ever happened again.

That was our private opinion too. Convinced that the CSM was carrying out a policy without the major's approval, we had called this bluff, and got away with it. But there was not one of us who would have liked to take the same chance again. A hundred and twenty pairs of hands cleared up the mess in the hut with such gusto that within twenty minutes there was not a D Company man left in the camp.

From that time we felt a new confidence and maturity as though we had suddenly grown up. We were really men now, and Red Devils at that.

Early training with the 6th Airborne Division, which was stationed around Bulford and Larkhill, was largely on Salisbury Plain and consisted of three main categories, namely: general soldiering, weaponry and flying training.

The first, which was basic for all infantry battalions of the British Army, was planned to produce, as far as we Red Devils were concerned, a very much higher standard of personal fitness, endurance and initiative than was normally required. It consisted mainly of drill, both on the square and in the field, route and forced marches, and lectures with demonstrations on all aspects of land fighting. It was also designed to weed out the weaker elements, and a few of these fell by the wayside as time went on.

Weapon training covered the use and maintenance not only of those weapons with which the division was equipped but also of those used by the enemy. Our personal weapon was the Mark 4 Lee Enfield rifle, an updated version of the standard British rifle from 1914 to 1941 with a manually operated bolt action. We were trained to try to achieve the same rate of fire as the Americans with their Garand automatic rifles, actually an impossibility, yet we did attain a very high rate of rapid fire, though it was awkward if you happened to be left-handed, since the action was designed for use by right-handed men. The bayonet was of the "pig-sticker" type, only about nine inches long and under half an inch in diameter. In addition to its legitimate purpose it was very useful for opening cans of soup or beer and toasting bread over an open fire and would probably have been ideal for taking stones out of horses' hooves.

Platoon sergeants and section leaders were issued with a special version of the Sten sub-machine carbine, while the officers had the choice of the Webley .38 revolver or the Browning FN automatic pistol which latter was also issued to specialists such as mortar-men and anti-tank gunners.

Training in the use of these personal weapons and the German and Italian equivalents such as the Luger and Walther pistols and the Schmeisser and Beretta sub-machine carbines which used the same ammunition as the Brownings and Stens made one feel that the arms firms had come to a pre-war arrangement on standardizing ammunition so that they would do well out of any conflict no matter which side won. Anyway, more than one German soldier was killed by a German weapon and ammunition in our hands, and I daresay the reverse was true. We had to be capable, in case of a stoppage, of stripping down all these automatic weapons and reassembling them blindfolded. More than once when campaigning I was grateful for this training.

Each section had a Bren light machine-gun which was fairly simple to operate, though compared to the German equivalent, the MG 42, it had only about half the rate of fire but was less likely to jam. The German gun needed the constant attention of a two-man team while the Bren was individually operated.

One of our easier days during this training period was that on which we visited the rifle range, which

35

happened about once a month. We fired from a series of marked positions, starting at a hundred yards and finishing at a thousand, with the final test at maximum range, in gas masks, at snap targets which were on view for only two or three seconds at a time. Every man was graded as a first-class or second-class marks-man, and anyone failing to achieve a sufficient score as the latter was immediately punished, being confined to barracks until he improved. However, with the threat of penalties hanging over them, most of the men achieved the necessary scores. For those who did not, their friends in the butts helped them out. Their work was to raise and lower the targets and paste small pieces of linen paper over the bullet holes. They also had to write in pencil the score on each firer's card. Fortunately it was soon realized that, when a bullet goes through a card, it leaves the same sort of mark as if the target had been stabbed by a pencil — a subterfuge also used to help the Bren-gunners.

I well remember one day, when we were getting ready for Bren-gun firing, an unfortunate rabbit which dashed across the range. The immediate reaction was a burst of fire, and the rabbit was reduced to a scattering of blood, fur and bones. Investigation revealed that once again the incorrigible Frank Bailey was the culprit.

Firing practice with Sten-guns, revolvers and pistols was carried out at a much shorter range on targets representing men. Even at fifty yards it is difficult to obtain any hits, let alone in the killing zones marked on the figure, with a Sten-gun which tends to move sideways and upwards as the burst is fired. As for the revolvers and pistols, a hit in the torso at twenty yards was considered a very good shot. We were taught to hold the pistols with our right hand pressing down on our left forearm, then take careful aim, hold our breath and squeeze the trigger slowly and firmly without snatching. All very different from the quick-draw stars of the Western movies.

In addition to these small arms, each platoon was issued with a two-inch-diameter mortar which was carried by one man and had a range of about a quarter of a mile. As there was no sight on it, we had to try to hit the target by trial and error, and although one man was designated as platoon mortarman, everyone had to know how to handle it.

The big brother of the two-inch mortar was the three-inch mortar, two of which were issued to each company. This was the heavy artillery of the Red Devils. It took a lot of muscle power to carry them around even when dismantled into the three sections, each of which weighed forty or fifty pounds. The members of the mortar team carried one of these sections, plus three bombs which weighed ten pounds each, but nevertheless they were among the luckier Red Devils since whenever possible jeeps and trailers were made available to carry the load. However, the final act in the three-inch-mortar course was what was known as the "long carry", a route march of ten miles with the mortar, a case of three bombs and all personal arms and ammunition were carried, a total of over ninety pounds per man of awkwardly shaped equipment.

If the three-inch mortar was the Red Devils' heavy artillery, our main anti-tank weapon was the PIAT, standing for Projectile Infantry Anti Tank, which we were told would knock out any known tank. Later, to our cost, we discovered that the newer enemy tanks were proof against even the PIAT. Each platoon was issued with one which, together with its ammunition, that for the two-inch mortar and other equipment, such as camouflage nets, was carried in the platoon handcart and went in the glider with us. Apart from the handcart load, everything else was carried by us beasts of burden.

As summer moved into autumn, and autumn into winter, we had a good deal of practice in demolitions in the woods on Salisbury Plain. Our company second-in-command, Captain "Pongo" Trelawney, used to take us out with two objectives, one being to teach us how to use explosives for demolitions and the other to see that the trees which were the subject of these practices were taken back to camp for firewood.

To fell a tree, Pongo would take a slab of gun cotton which was quite inert and therefore safe to handle, and insert a primary charge in the pre-formed hole in the centre. He would then place the end of a length of fuse into a detonator, crimping them together with his teeth — if he had been a quarter of an inch out and bitten the detonator, he would have blown his head off. He would then slide the detonator into the hole in the primary charge, tie the complete device to the trunk of the tree just above ground level with the length of fuse and after setting this alight withdraw out of danger. As often as not, down came the tree. He used the same technique with equal effect on railway tracks and later taught us how to make bombs from gelignite, with petrol cans, bottles and just about any kind of container that came to hand. When, however, it was our turn to prepare the demolition charges, he would not let us crimp the detonators in our teeth but made us use a special pair of pliers. Once, when he was not about, Frank Bailey could not resist the temptation of crimping one with his teeth and, as usual, got away with it.

Pongo was a big, tall Cornishman, with a shock of ginger hair and an impressively wide RAF-style moustache, hence his nickname as to us all, RAF officers being known as Pongos. He was a bit of an eccentric, was absolutely fearless when handling explosives, had a good sense of humour and made soldiering almost enjoyable. Needless to say, we all thought a lot of him.

Throwing live grenades, from a pit, for the first time was another rather frightening experience. The Mills grenade, the Army's standard anti-personnel grenade, was designed to fit snugly into the hand for throwing while the detonator was kept in a "safe" position by a lever held against the grenade by the hand and also secured by a pin. Once the pin was withdrawn and the pressure on the lever released, the grenade would explode within five seconds. Four or five of us were allowed in the pit at a time, and each man in turn aimed for the target, withdrew the pin with his other hand, threw the grenade over-arm style like bowling a

39

cricket ball, noted where it landed and then ducked quickly into the pit.

Sergeant Bert Walters warned us against panic if anything went wrong; the thing to do was to stand still. Sure enough, one of the men in our group dropped a live grenade as he was about to throw. The sergeant yelled to us to stand still and was down on the grenade like greased lightning. He may not have been much of an athlete, but he moved like one getting that grenade out of the pit before it exploded.

Clearing minefields and defusing booby traps were other skills we had to learn. The mines and booby traps we practised on were fitted with only a detonator, which gave off a bang like a firecracker when set off, but we knew that the penalty in action would be the loss of life or limb. The fine for setting off a detonator was one shilling — a quarter of a day's pay or the price of a pint of bitter — so no one could afford to set off too many in a morning's session. The golden rule was that, if a man trod on a mine, he had to keep his foot on it until someone else removed the detonator. If he came up against a loose trip-wire, he did not pull it; if a tight wire, he did not cut it. Booby traps required very careful examination in order to locate and neutralize the detonator and thus save the evening's beer money.

Life was very tough in the Airborne Division, but by this time we were revelling in our physical fitness. We were happy enough, though most of us would not have admitted it, and we had some time off. One week we would train for 6½ days, with only a twelve-hour pass out on the Sunday afternoon. In the next week we would train for only 5½ days and have a thirty-six-hour pass out at the week-end. The men who could not get home or, more likely, did not want to, used the thirty-six hours in their fortnightly escapade to "The Smoke" — London. Most of us could not afford tickets and so had to get past the station by force or guile, the ensuing Battle of Waterloo being regularly repeated at fortnightly intervals.

The standard Sunday-night joke as the men returned to camp was to ask our few married men, "And what was the second thing you did when you got home?" "Took off my pack and greatcoat," was the unvarying reply. It got a laugh every time.

CHAPTER
FIVE

Flying Training

And so to flying. The other companies had already done theirs, and so now it was the turn of us newcomers. We had learnt that in the parachute battalions you received your wings after ten drops. In a glider or air landing brigade you earned them after four hours' flying training in a glider. We were to find that four hours in a glider can be a very long time, especially for a novice.

It was in the middle of an August heat-wave when the advance party of which I was one reported to Company HQ and loaded our kit onto a three-ton truck for the two hours cross-country trip to the RAF station at Brize Norton in Oxfordshire. Arriving there, we settled into the hut reserved to us and were immediately given the rest of the day off. Sergeant Dixie Howard who was i/c of our small group went off to the sergeants' mess after giving us orders to get our breakfast next day at the RAF "sprogs" mess at eight o'clock and then report for duty at nine o'clock.

Eight o'clock! Nine o'clock! On Salisbury Plain we would have been halfway through our morning programme by then. And better still, no clocking on or off when leaving the airfield, no roll-call and in the mess actually a choice of food! It seemed too good to be true, and we wondered whether we were still fighting the same war. However, there was nothing to be lost by making the best of the good life while it lasted.

Another novelty. For the first time on a military establishment we found girls, WAAFs — Women's Auxiliary Air Force — as well as men. In no time at all we found ourselves girl friends to whom it seemed that having twelve budding Red Devils on the airfield was a new experience — and one they liked. Then there were film shows, dances in the villages and a new set of local pubs to be tested.

I remember that in one of the villages, early in our course, there was a fairground in full swing. One of the attractions was to climb on a platform about thirty feet above the ground, grab a handle attached to a pulley wheel on a wire and shoot down this to land in a big pile of hay. There was a safety net under the wire in case of accident.

The first of our gang to have a go was "Tosser" Barnes, a special friend of mine who had been a farmer's boy. He had not gone more than five yards down the wire before he let go of the handle and plummeted into the safety net, which promptly collapsed. Down went the supporting poles, and Tosser finished on the ground wrapped up in the safety net and underneath a pile of poles and guy ropes. The silly ass had been under the impression that landing in the safety net was the object of the exercise. He must have thought he was back at camp in training. Anyway the old fairground barker would not let any more of us have a go.

We then persuaded Joe French, also a farmer's boy, to ride one of the fairground horses bareback, since he reckoned he could do so without being thrown. He was right! To a chorus of catcalls and slapping of the horse's rump, he shot out of the fairground and up the lane. He did not fall off; neither could he get off or stop the horse, and it was a good four hours later when we saw him again. By that time all the pubs had closed, and we had taken our girl friends home.

There were plenty of barns and hayricks in Oxfordshire, a good proportion of them on our way to camp. There never seemed to be any hurry to get back and no trouble there on our arrival. However, it came as a bit of a shock when we learnt that some of the WAAFs were parachute packers, when they teasingly warned us not to let them down or upset them as we needed their parachutes if anything went wrong with the gliders.

Back at the camp on Salisbury Plain, Sergeant Dixie Howard had been a disciplinarian. But it would have been very difficult to enforce our usual spartan living standards in the present surroundings, so he felt compelled to allow discipline to relax except for when we were actually on duty, and all in all they were very pleasant surroundings in which to carry out our flying training.

Our party had been allocated one ancient Armstrong Whitworth Whitley bomber and a Horsa glider. The bomber had a crew of two, pilot and observer, and the glider one, the pilot. On our second morning we reported for duty and set off on our first flight. The Whitley, towing the glider, edged forward, took up the slack in the tow rope and then opened throttle and roared along the runway. We twelve sat tight, particularly so because the glider door had been left open, just for the effect. Up we went, following the plane about a hundred yards behind it and a few feet above its slipstream. We thought it a marvellous sensation, and it did not take us long to reach the stage of bravado when we would stand in the doorway of the glider and look down at the fields beneath us. This first time we flew around for an hour or so. Then back over the airfield the glider pilot cast off the tow rope and brought the glider in to land. The technique was to bring the glider down at a very sharp angle and level out at the last moment before hitting the ground so that it would come to a halt within one hundred yards of landing.

For the rest of the morning we had to practise loading and unloading the glider from the front and the rear. "Speed", said the pilot "is absolutely vital." A glider towed by an aeroplane at one hundred miles an hour is an easy target for ack-ack and ground fire, but once it has landed, it is many times more vulnerable. It was imperative that the glider was loaded in such a way that there was no delay in unloading, or if necessary so that we could temporarily abandon the least vital pieces of equipment.

We spent the afternoon doing short trips, so that we got used to the routine of landing and taking off. After the third flight the glider pilot asked if one of us would like to lend a hand, since it was rather windy and he needed some help to control the glider. I jumped at it, and the pilot explained the controls, which were simple enough. The two foot-pedals controlled the rudder and therefore our sideways movements, and the joystick, which was in front of me and between my knees, determined whether we went up or down. By the feel of the dual controls I was able to pick it up in a few minutes and was just beginning to feel very pleased with myself when the pilot told me to take over. We would not be casting off the tow rope for some while, so he was going to enjoy a quiet smoke.

We learned later that it was standard practice for one of us to act as co-pilot during this training period, but I was taken by surprise, and I doubt if ever a novice pilot felt more jittery, though I expect those behind had even less confidence in my ability, but their turn had yet to come. There was little cause for apprehension, for the pilot, having enjoyed his cigarette and his little joke, took over again before we cast off the rope and came in to land.

After two weeks of pleasant days of flying and even more pleasant evenings with the WAAFs, our holiday was over when the rest of D Company arrived and discipline was back to normal. We twelve were given our wings and immediately recruited as observers in the rear turrets of the tow planes.

A five-minute briefing from the pilot of the Whitley as we walked across the tarmac to the aircraft before take-off was the only instruction I received as "tail-end

Charlie". "If you want to talk to me, just put on the head phones and call long-distance," he cracked. "Remember, you're my second pair of eyes. They haven't thought of putting wing mirrors on these old planes, so we need a tail-end Charlie."

The rear turret of the aircraft is one of the loneliest places in the world, and sitting there for hours on end, especially at night, is an ordeal. Fortunately our flying was being done over Britain, and nobody was shooting at us, but a few flights in the rear turret were sufficient to give us a deep respect for the air gunners in our bombers over Germany.

While I was clambering along the fuselage into the rear gunner's turret, the pilot was warming up the two engines. The ground crew removed the chocks, and the Whitley slowly eased forward until the slack in the tow rope was taken up; then I had to report that the glider was ready for take-off. The old Whitley then moved off at full power until it attained a speed of about one hundred miles an hour and the glider had lifted six or eight feet off the ground. "Glider airborne," I shouted. That told the pilot it was safe to take off, and soon we were droning over the countryside with the glider sailing along behind. I sat watching it and thinking that last week I had been sitting there; now it held a full complement of thirty men and, in a way, I had some responsibility for their lives.

It always seemed an interminable time by day, and twice as long by night, before we were back over the airfield and ready for the glider to cast off. Released, the Whitley would then circle the airfield preparatory to

47

dropping the tow rope in an adjacent field where a team of RAF "sprogs", as the other ranks were called, were waiting with a truck to pick it up. Try as we might, we never managed to score a direct hit on the truck with the tow rope, though we were always in the right field and had the sprogs running for cover now and again.

The last evening at the airfield most of us went out on a drinking party with some WAAFs. It was a memorable night, but the morning dawned black and bleak. I could take no breakfast other than a mug of steaming black coffee and then had to do no fewer than eight flights as tail-end Charlie, being alternately sick and sorry, which cost me 5 shillings. The rule was that you either cleaned up the consequences yourself or paid the ground crew to do it, which at this time I thought cheap at the price.

There had been one upsetting development when Ginger Thompson, who was the smallest man in D Company, proved to be dead scared of flying and we had to lift him, kicking and screaming, into the glider for every flight. If he had refused to fly, he would have been liable to a court martial as, like the rest of us, he was supposed to be a volunteer. Later we were to wonder whether it would not have been wiser to leave him alone, for he was killed during the Normandy landings.

Although by this time we were becoming hardened and, to some extent, tough, experienced soldiers, as Red Devils should be, most of us, like myself, still had several months to go before our nineteenth birthdays.

CHAPTER
SIX

"In Bed or Out of Barracks"

Glider training over, we returned to general training on Salisbury Plain, and until we flew into action, we never entered a glider again except when taking part in special exercises. The days passed with more weapon training, battle drill, route marches, map-reading, initiative and endurance tests, manœuvres and, of course, sport.

One of the battalion's favourite sports was "Shrove Tuesday" football. A whole company, including officers and NCOs, would be divided into two roughly equal teams, which meant there were sixty or so men on each side. The game was played on a football pitch, with one football, and there were no rules! Each side had to try to get the ball into the other team's goal by whatever means possible, and the game generally lasted most of the afternoon, with many an old score settled during it.

Lieutenant Guthrie, who had arrived to take command of 31 platoon, once, unwisely, held onto the ball in one of the scrummages. Not only did he get rather mauled in the mêlée but he lost one of his boots and played the rest of the game with one sock hanging off. Inevitably from that time forward he was known as "Flannelfoot" Guthrie. Sergeant-Major Bill Maynard and Quartermaster-Sergeant Jem Hacker were always in the thick of the conflict, as other ranks tried to have a go at them, but they were able to look after themselves and always emerged in reasonably good shape.

The time had now arrived for D Company to be put on a full establishment. First and second lieutenants had been drafted in as platoon commanders, and the only gaps that needed to be filled were the section seconds-in-command, who would be given the rank of lance-corporal. The lance-corporal is the lowest form of Army life above the private soldier and indeed is even usually looked down upon by the latter. Nevertheless, as the rank carried a rise in pay, Frank, Tiger and myself were all quite pleased to be selected for promotion. We were separated, Frank and I going into different assault platoons, while Tiger, with his usual luck, was drafted to the Company three-inch-mortar section.

Airborne assault platoons were split into three sections, each commanded by a corporal armed with a Sten-gun. Under him were five riflemen including a sniper who, because of his prowess on the rifle range, was given a rifle with a telescopic sight. The corporal in charge of my section was Joe Boston, a small, chirpy man in his late twenties. He was married and lived in the Devon town of Okehampton, which was sufficient reason for him to be given the nickname of Woodcock

— though not to his face. He was a little terrier of a man and a great patrol leader, and although he was only about five foot three in height, nobody ever dared to take liberties with him. The men were sure that the furtive, wary look on his ferret-like face was due to long years as a poacher on the fringe of Dartmoor. There was not a man in the company who could match his stealth and cunning on a night patrol; he seemed to come and go in the dark like some prowling night creature, never seen or heard. He had, however, the failing of many small men: he was too aggressive, even for the Red Devils whose aggression had to be tinged with caution, and eventually this failing cost him his life in action.

The rest of the section consisted of myself, as lance-corporal, armed with a rifle, the Bren-gunner and his number two, who also carried a rifle as well as spare ammunition for the Bren-gun. My Bren-gunner was Joe French, and his number two was Bill Simpson. Joe, although only of medium height, was tremendously thickset and stocky and was as strong as one of his farm horses. He got the job because of his capacity for trench-digging. Whenever we stopped while on an exercise, the first job was to dig a slit trench, and it did not take me long to realize that Joe could dig a trench faster than any man in the platoon with very little help from anyone else. Bill was a big, strapping, amiable lad whose parents kept a pub down near the dockyard at Plymouth. He was quite a good boxer, though how he ever managed to get involved in boxing I could not fathom, for he was such a friendly giant that I could not imagine him hurting anyone. He came in for quite a lot of good-natured banter, even from Sergeant Walters, who one day pulled him out for not shaving.

"But I did shave, Sarge," said Bill plaintively.

"Did you have to share a mirror then?"

"Yes, Sarge."

"Then you must have shaved someone else's face," said Sergeant Walters.

Bill was very popular. He, Joe and I stuck together for the rest of our training period and went into action as a team in the Normandy landings. It was Bill who met his death in that treacherous attack in the orchard at Breville.

We continued perfecting our battle drill. Its essence was always to attack, which usually culminated in a bayonet charge, where we were taught to scream at the top of our voices, run like mad and stick our bayonets into sacks suspended in the air, representing bodies. We then had to withdraw our bayonet immediately and continue the charge until we had overcome all resistance. Our instructions were never to have our rifles loaded, as we were supposed to kill the enemy with the bayonet rather than shoot him. In action this order was ignored by many of us who had already decided, in the training stage, that we would rather shoot a Jerry than run him through with a "pig-sticker".

In defence, we were exhorted never to retreat, which was sound enough advice, for in an airborne operation there was usually nowhere to retreat to. We were told always to fight to the last round of ammunition and never surrender. In the unlikely event of our being taken prisoner, it was our first duty to escape. Our training was certainly comprehensive and thorough. Map-reading was obviously of the highest importance, since, with the best will and skill in the world, the gliders rarely landed on the intended target, so the first thing we had to do on landing was to find out just where we were and make for our objective.

To test this training, we would be dropped at night from sealed trucks in various parts of Salisbury Plain and told to find our way to a rendezvous point for which we had been given a map reference. It was on these exercises that Joe Boston and I achieved considerable fame as map-readers and navigators. We worked out a dependable system, the essential part of which was that I had to sit in the back of the truck with a map and a small torch, following our route by checking the outside countryside as seen through a tiny gap we had made in the canvas cover. When our section was dropped off, we knew exactly where we were and had only to take a compass bearing and then march straight to our objective. It was usually a journey of three or four miles, so by midnight we would be comfortably bedded down in our sleeping-bags while other groups would still be wandering about the country-side. Some would not arrive until breakfast time and then had to be ready to carry on with the exercise immediately. Try as they might, the officers never discovered the secret of why our section was always first at the rendezvous. In the end they put it down to Joe's poacher's instinct and his ability to see in the dark. No one in the section, of course, ever split, and some of them did not even know what was happening; they just followed, hoping that their leaders knew what they were doing.

The exercises gradually developed into attacks on limited objectives, such as railway or river bridges, which were defended by "enemy" troops. Umpires would judge the results of the attack and tie labels on "casualties". If the enemy was drafted from our own company or battalion, there was rarely any trouble, but if from any of the other battalions the attacks would become much more realistic, usually ending in hand-to-hand fighting. Rifles and bayonets would be thrown to the ground, and the men would fight with bare fists, watched by the officers who remained passive until things showed signs of getting out of hand. These dust-ups resulted in the first-aid men, who were the stretcher-bearers, having some real patients to deal with, as well as the imaginary as labelled by the umpires.

In due course the exercises became longer, spreading over three or four days. We soon learned how to make ourselves as comfortable as possible in all types of weather conditions by building bivouacs as shelter from any rain at night. Sometimes we would be issued with individual ration packs which had to last the full period of the exercise, and on others rations were brought up which we often had to cook for ourselves, though sometimes a field kitchen would be set up. On these occasions the menu was invariably stew, and how delicious it tasted after long hours in the open air, followed up by plum duff. The quartermaster, Jem

Hacker, would serve only one portion of duff to each man, and those who wanted a second helping, which usually included the whole company, had to form a large circle around the surplus plum duff placed on the grass. At a signal from Hacker a hundred men dashed in and fought, kicked and battered each other until all the food was gone. It was all good fun and we enjoyed it, especially if we had managed to grab a handful of duff.

Back in camp, the training now included unarmed combat — how to defend ourselves unarmed against an enemy with a rifle and bayonet; how to kill a man with our bare hands; how to kill a man with one thrust of a knife, and many other tricks of our so-called trade.

Life was busy all the time; every hour of the day and sometimes of the night was filled with activity. In the evenings, when there were no duties or training, the golden rule was: "In bed or out of barracks". I had learnt that rule when one Saturday afternoon I was sitting on my bed as the PT sergeant came in the room.

"Ever played Rugby League, son?" he asked.

"No, Sarge."

"Ah, I remember, you played for us at soccer last week. You'll do."

"Do what, Sarge?"

"We're a man short, and we're playing the locals at Rugby this afternoon, and now you're in the team."

I protested but an order was an order.

As I sat in the bath with the rest of the team after the game, aching and bruised all over, the PT sergeant said, "Remember in future, son, when off duty the idea is — in bed or out of barracks."

I never forgot that lesson.

All through the winter of 1943-4 the training continued, and the officers were continually thinking up new ideas to keep us busy and prevent us from becoming stale. One of them hit upon the notion of stranding us all, in twos and threes, on Dartmoor, without any money or rail tickets and instructions to get back to Salisbury Plain as quickly as possible. We could use whatever means we liked and had only one rule — any man caught stealing or committing a civil offence would be punished under civil law and further be liable to an army charge for bringing the service into disrepute. It was a good initiative test, except that the civilian population were more helpful and co-operative than we could expect in an occupied country, and Joe, Bill and I were usually back in camp within forty-eight hours. I remember we spent one night in a flour mill and the whole of the next morning beating flour out of our uniforms. The next night we slept as guests in Devizes police station.

Back at camp we were treated to occasional film shows. One, that must have been nearly worn into tatters by continual showing, was called *Next of Kin* and was a security film showing how a chance remark in a family circle enabled the enemy to find out in advance about a commando raid, as a result of which many troops were lost. Another was one about the effects of VD; inevitably it was called by us *Next to Skin*.

Once a week, as a break from exercises and other training, we were taken on a route march. In spite of the fact that we usually footslogged between thirty and thirty-five miles, which took ten to twelve hours, we looked upon this as one of the easier days of the week, especially in fine weather. We had nothing to do but march, sing Army songs and swop stories. Every platoon had its joker, and ours was Ken Edwards. He knew the biggest collection of filthy songs that any of us had ever heard and was able to carry on cracking blue Army jokes all day without repeating himself.

Sport also played a large part in our training schedules, and my own particular favourite was cross-country running. I found out later, when I was in hospital after being wounded, that I had an athlete's heart in that my pulse rate was only about fifty to the minute instead of the normal seventy-two. The doctors told me that this was a big help in long-distance running; anyhow I made the battalion team which won the 6th Airborne Division championship that year, and later my ability to run fast and keep running was to serve me even better, as without it I would hardly have survived.

Also in the team was a Somerset lad, Ron Spence, who, weight for weight, was also probably the best boxer in the battalion, being a big, strong and we all thought fearless lad. As it turned out, he was the only deserter D Company ever had. It happened about a week before D-Day; he just disappeared and nobody in the company ever heard of him again. It came as a bad shock to us all. If any of us had had to pick a fellow

57

soldier likely to desert it would have been Jack Rawlings, who was the worst soldier in the company but who, to our surprise, went on to win the Military Medal in Normandy. We all thought it must have been fear with Ron, for although we were not told the date of D-Day, he knew, as we did, that it was not very far off.

Boxing was almost as popular as cross-country running in the battalion, and we had some very good boxers in the company, including Ron Spence and Bill Simpson. The main problem with boxing in the Army was that you rarely had a chance to learn much about the form of your opponents, particularly those from other units, and during one tournament I was very surprised to see Bill get knocked out in the first round from a seemingly harmless blow. By one of the strange coincidences of Army life I was later to share a hut at a convalescent camp with a corporal from another unit in the division. This man had been a professional boxer and asked if I knew Bill and then told me that, although he realized Bill was a game lad, he was way out of his depth in this contest and in a clinch suggested that the next time he hit him Bill should take a dive or he would finish up getting hurt. Bill had done the sensible thing, as I was to do myself later on; I did not mind being outclassed on the soccer field by professional footballers but being hurt in the boxing ring was a bit different, so after a few tentative experiences in the ring I opted out whenever possible.

This I managed to do reasonably well, except from collective boxing, one of CSM Bill Maynard's more sadistic pastimes. He would rope off a square about double the size of a boxing ring, put the whole platoon into it with their gloves on and declare that the last man left standing was the winner. To add to the interest of these contests he decreed that everyone had to be blindfolded. The last two or three men on their feet could find their opponents only from the instructions bawled by the rest of the company.

The climax of our training drew near. In a dress rehearsal for D-Day we flew gliders about halfway across the Channel and then returned to England. One glider from A Company somehow got lost and landed its occupants complete with blank ammunition in occupied France, where they were all taken prisoner. When later I met one of the survivors, who had spent about a year in a POW camp, he told me that for a time the Germans thought that the Second Front had started.

This particular exercise was the one and only time that we flew in American WACO gliders, towed by American planes, and we were all pleased that it was the last. The method of takeoff and flying was entirely different to that of the RAF. The planes and gliders would be lined up side by side on the runway with the tow rope coiled up between them. As one plane was leaving the ground, the next would move off, soon reaching what appeared to be maximum speed and jerking the glider violently forward; if we had not been strapped in, there would have been some nasty casualties before we had even left the ground. The plane would then drag the glider off the ground, towing it below its slipstream; I could not understand why we always flew above the slipstream and the Americans below — presumably personal preferences of the top brass.

This exercise was fraught with incidents. Not only did that glider stray and land in France but one of D Company's gliders came down when the tow rope broke over the Channel about twenty miles off the English coast. The survivors were picked up by the RAF air-sea rescue service after they had been sitting on the wing for about half an hour and only minutes before the glider sank, but one man was drowned and six or seven were injured. The fatality was Bill Coombes, eighteen years old!

Next day CSM Maynard carried out his usual roll-call.

"Coombes," he barked.

"Coombes," he yelled.

"He's dead, sir," somebody said.

"Well, that's just as well, or he'd have been on a charge for AWOL," shouted the bastard Maynard.

The target of this exercise was an airfield defended by the resident RAF regiment and the local Home Guard. As usual in a populated countryside we used only blank ammunition, but for similar exercises on Dartmoor and Exmoor we were issued with the real stuff, as we continued to gain experience in handling all our weapons, including flame-throwers which we did not like at all, wishing that both sides would ban the use of them. Nobody can play with fire without somebody getting hurt, and we had quite a few casualties but no other fatalities.

Every event in our training now reminded us that the big day was rapidly approaching, and none of us was surprised when the order to move was given. We were taken to a camp in Essex, and on arrival the gates were closed against the outside world. For some, indeed, the gates were closed on the outside world forever.

CHAPTER
SEVEN

D-Day

The first thing we learned when we arrived at the staging camp in Essex at the end of May 1944 was that the rest of the battalion were not there, and we were told that there were not enough gliders or tow planes to take the whole battalion across the Channel. So D Company, as the junior company, was to travel to the Second Front by boat. This was a big disappointment, particularly as we had had no training in assaulting beaches. Also it hurt our pride. We did not like being treated as younger brothers. However, our opinion was not asked for.

Sealed away from the outside world, with military police guarding the gates, we settled down to our new role and absorbed the briefing for "Operation Overlord", the invasion of north-west Europe.

We learned that the landings were to take place in Normandy, on the beaches between the River Orne and the Cherbourg peninsula. The 6th Airborne Division were to land and capture and hold the bridgehead on the east of the River Orne, thus protecting the otherwise exposed flank of the British 2nd Army, which, with the Canadian 1st Army, was responsible for the eastern half of the invasion coast, the western sector, towards Cherbourg being the objective of the American 1st and 3rd Armies.

Our briefing was detailed, with large-scale maps and plans, and we formed a reasonable idea of what was expected of us, both as a unit and as individuals. However, even with the best briefing in the world, things could not be expected to go entirely according to plan. Much depended on the Airborne troops landing on target, and sometimes they did not, when small groups of determined troops found themselves confronted with objectives for which the planning and briefing experts had reckoned on considerably larger forces. It happened all along the front in Normandy. At the Orne bridges for instance, of five gliders briefed, only two were on target. But the platoons from these two successfully captured the bridges before the enemy could demolish them.

After a few days of briefing, interspersed with football, boxing and any other activities the officers and NCOs could dream up to keep us happy within the confines of the camp, the order came to move. A convoy of trucks appeared to take us to Tilbury, about eight miles away. The bulk of our kit was left in camp, to be sent back to our depot on Salisbury Plain. We wore only our battledress and flying-smocks and carried our personal arms and grenades. Live ammunition, a hundred rounds per man, was issued. We were travelling light in readiness for the great assault.

It took us an hour to get to Tilbury, where, without delay, we embarked on landing-craft waiting at the quay. These, known as LCI (Landing Craft Infantry), had a naval crew, were lightly armed with anti-aircraft guns and had accommodation for about 120 men, the normal complement of a company. Bunks and hammocks were provided for all, but there was no spare space, and we were packed in like peas in a pod.

As the LCI left the quayside and nosed its way down the Thames estuary, on a blustery, overcast day with short, sharp waves tossing up white horses all around us, we were given our final briefings and learned that D-Day was 5th June, the next day but one. That meant, we quickly realized, that we would spend two days aboard the landing-craft.

The weather deteriorated. Several gales were lashing the English Channel, and D-Day was postponed for twenty-four hours, to 6th June, and we passed three very uncomfortable days zigzagging up and down the storm-tormented Channel. If the enemy were watching us, they must have found our antics highly confusing.

The landing-craft, being necessarily of shallow draft and having a blunt bow, did not cut through the waves at all but rode up them until the front third of the keel was out of water. Then, as if to right the balance, the boat would crash down into the trough, jarring us from stem to stern and throwing vast sheets of water over us. As the boat mounted the next wave, the rear third would quit the water with a terrific roar as the screws, threshing the air, raced at an accelerated speed until the hull dropped into the sea again. Our training had taught us never to be surprised at anything, but certainly being tossed about in a small boat in a wild sea had never entered our calculations. More than half of us were violently seasick, whilst those who felt capable of taking nourishment mastered the technique of eating our meals with one hand whilst gripping any handhold for dear life with the other. We learnt how to climb into a swaying hammock without immediately falling out on the other side and even managed to stay in it all night, though we got little sleep.

Perhaps it was as well that we had so many minor problems and discomforts to keep our minds off the dangers that lay ahead. During training the thought of going into action and the doubts about how we would face up to it were things we tried to put out of our minds. Indeed, with the successes on the Russian Front and in the Mediterranean, there always seemed a faint hope that a Second Front in the West might not be needed, so we never got further than vaguely thinking about it, and the subject was taboo in conversation.

Now that there was no doubt about its reality, we still did not discuss our fears with each other. Instead, we engaged in interminable games of poker, brag and pontoon, as far as the antics of the boat would allow, and there were even schools of housey-housey going on, now popularly called Bingo, this being the only gambling game officially permitted in the Army. Some of us managed to write letters to our families, and these we left with the crew, for posting when the landing-craft returned to Britain.

In spite of these activities and the unending struggle for handholds and footholds to prevent us being tossed about and injured, the time passed very slowly. It seemed an age before, finally, D-Day dawned. The morning light revealed a sea that was still looking spiteful and wicked. The sky was overcast, and a strong wind was blowing. All around us were ships like ours, heading south. We could now plainly hear the rumble of gunfire ashore and the deafening roar of the guns of cruisers and battleships lying offshore. They were, of course, providing long-range support for the unlucky devils in the first wave of the invasion forces.

Fortunately the Allies had air superiority over the beach-heads, and we could see RAF Spitfires and Typhoons going in at what seemed to be mast height to fire their rockets and cannon shells. As our landing-craft neared the coast, the noise became more continuous and deafening. The land could hardly be seen through a pall of smoke that hung over what was now a battlefield.

A mile or two off the beaches, we took up our positions, waiting for the boat to ground in shallow water. The first wave of assault troops had landed from conventional invasion barges, fed from larger ships standing offshore, under the protection of the Navy. As the barges touched the beach, their front sections were lowered, making it possible for the men to land without even getting their feet wet — if they were lucky. The LCIs, on the other hand, being larger boats, though still with a shallow draft, had to ease towards shore until they grounded in three or four feet of water. The men then had to disembark by gangways on both sides of the bow, jump into the surf and make their way ashore. The leading man carried a rope with him, to act as a safety line for those following, and our instructions were to leap into the water as soon as the order was given and wade ashore without letting go of the safety line. Once there, we were to get off the beach as fast as we could.

During the last half-hour before landing, I sat silently on my haunches, trying to analyse my thoughts. Naturally I was afraid, but I was not going to show it. If I was going to die, I hoped it would be quick and that I would know nothing about it. Contrary to a common belief, I did not think about my family, home or past life; I was much more concerned lest, in the face of the enemy, I would turn out to be a coward and let the other men and myself down. Also I was afraid of being wounded and perhaps losing a limb. Here again, though, my chief fear was that I might not be able to bear the pain and break down before my comrades. The training we had received accentuated these natural fears since we knew that, as a *corps d'élite*, we must not let each other down.

A shudder went through the boat as it touched the sandy bottom, a few yards from shore. I said a silent prayer: "Please God, make me a good soldier, and help me to come out of this alive." As I finished praying I heard the order: "Come on. Down you go and get off that bloody beach."

When it came to my turn, I scrambled from the gangway, waited for a split second for a wave to go by

67

and then, clutching the safety line with one hand, jumped up to my armpits in the surf, my rifle held high over my head with the other hand. I struggled safely ashore, as did all the men in my platoon. We could see, though, that other platoons had not been so lucky. There were bodies floating on the tide. Evidently some of them had not held on to their safety lines and had been dragged down by the weight of their equipment, or they had been shot by snipers in their most vulnerable moments.

Arriving on the beaches of Normandy without a single casualty was a matter for elation and relief, and we began to feel pleased with ourselves, but the feeling was not to last for long. The commandos and the others in the first wave of troops had knocked out the shore batteries and machine-gun posts overlooking the beaches but not all the snipers, who appeared to be in church towers, farmhouses and any buildings commanding a good range of vision. We would have liked to isolate them, surround each one and wipe them out, but our orders were to press on to the Orne bridges. So we largely ignored them, returning fire only now and then to make them keep their heads down and prevent their becoming too bold.

Even then I realized that, unless we were careful, we would soon run out of ammunition, as I had already expended twenty rounds or so, and I knew that Joe French had been even busier with the Bren-gun. To run out of ammunition so early in the battle would be disastrous, and goodness knows, I thought, when or how further supplies are going to get to us. I soon found the answer. Under a hedge I came upon the first dead man of D Company — a lad from another platoon, whom I knew only slightly. I steeled myself to bend over the body, not more than ten minutes dead, and removed the two bandoliers, one from each shoulder. Now I had another hundred rounds of precious ammunition, which fitted both the rifles and the Bren-gun, and it soon became standard practice to replenish our supplies in this way.

We had landed on the beach at about noon, and by late afternoon we reached the Orne bridges which were already in our hands, so we pressed on and linked up with the rest of the battalion. With them we advanced for a further two or three miles, until eventually deployed in a defensive position on the perimeter of the bridgehead.

My platoon was allotted a farmhouse and outbuildings for a defensive post, which we fortified as best we could. As it happened, we now had a respite, for the enemy had been taken by surprise and had not yet been able to mount a counterattack, so we had time to deal with the snipers. We winkled them out, for the rest of that evening and most of the next day. Joe Boston spotted the first one up a tree after a rifle bullet had passed dangerously close to us. Borrowing a rifle with a telescopic sight, he took a shot at about three hundred yards and knocked him out of the tree. If the man was not killed by the bullet, he certainly was when he hit the ground.

Meantime, things were happening over our heads. Throughout D-Day and the two or three that followed, the Allied Air Forces had been able to maintain air supremacy over the battlefields, but now the enemy had sufficiently recovered to challenge them. For the next day or two the RAF and the Luftwaffe shared the skies over our sector, and it was decided to give us anti-aircraft support, so a section of the Royal Artillery with a Bofors gun was sent to join us. Unfortunately the crew had had next to no training in aircraft recognition and tended to let fly at every plane that passed overhead, regardless of which side it belonged to. As a result, our farmhouse was soon being strafed by both the Luftwaffe and the RAF.

I had always been keen on aircraft spotting, right from my schooldays in the East End, during the Blitz and while the Battle of Britain was raging overhead, and was familiar with most types of both British and German planes. So Sergeant Walters arranged for my section to be stationed nearest the anti-aircraft gun and to take over its fire control — a popular arrangement, as thereafter we were strafed only by the Germans.

CHAPTER
EIGHT

The Fortified
Farmyard

We stayed in our farmhouse for the second and third days, gradually improving its fortifications between enemy attacks, which increased in number and strength as the Germans brought up reserves. It was during one of these attacks that for the first time I got a German in my rifle sights. I held my breath, squeezed the trigger exactly as I had been taught, and down he went. Whether he was dead or not I did not know, and I had no time to think about it, for others were coming at us, shouting.

The attack which came nearest to success was one which reached the farmyard gate on the flank of our position. We engaged in a spirited small-arms battle across the yard until Lieutenant Guthrie personally led a charge which drove the Germans out. We took two wounded prisoners and chased the rest away. It was then that our poacher, little Joe Boston, allowed his aggressiveness to upset his judgement. Instead of remaining in the farmyard, he started off in pursuit of the enemy and was cut down fifty yards from cover. We could do nothing but watch him die from several bursts of machine-gun fire. We were not even able to send out a stretcher party to retrieve the body until after nightfall.

The countryside in that part of Normandy is undulating, with small fields and many hedges and ditches, not at all the sort of country that tank commanders like as there are far too many obstacles. The German Panzers were no doubt frustrated at having to confine their manœuvres more to the lanes than the fields, though on some occasions this helped them rather than us.

It was during an early morning attack that a tank crept up a winding lane on our flank and suddenly appeared quite near the farmhouse. The following tank was crippled by our anti-tank gunners, blocking the lane so that no more could get through, but the leading one was in a position to do all the damage that was necessary.

As it trundled along the lane towards the farmhouse, Jack Rawlings, our PIAT mortar-man, jumped up out of his slit trench and went chasing after it. When he judged he was near enough, he stopped and fired his mortar from the hip. The shell penetrated the tank, which had lighter armour at the rear and knocked it out. He was awarded the Military Medal on the battlefield, the first but by no means the last decoration to be won by men of our company. It was ironical that at the time he was under open arrest, having been found asleep at his post by the Company Commander on the previous evening, and was awaiting court martial. He was not, by Army standards, a good soldier, and his brave deed seemed out of character. A tall, skinny lad, he was scruffy in appearance and a constant irritation to Sergeant Bert Walters, who during training had to keep chivvying him to keep him even moderately alert and tidy. Nothing further was heard about Rawlings' court martial, but he did not live long to enjoy his Military Medal as he was killed by a mortar bomb a few days later.

The episode of the tank caused us some anxiety. It was obvious that our six-pounders, which were the largest anti-tank guns that could be carried in gliders, were not sufficiently powerful to pierce their frontal armour. However, Pongo Trelawney was equal to the challenge. He showed us how to make a large grenade of gelignite, about six inches in diameter, with a detonator attached. We had to roll it along the road so that it went under the tank's tracks. It proved effective. From that time no enemy tank got through our lines.

Even in the front line, life was not all fighting and action. Attacks came mainly at dawn and dusk, and during the day we saw little of the enemy and hoped they had not seen us. However, the slightest movement between our slit trenches brought down a mortar barrage, and the Germans seemed to be particularly alert when a ration party was bringing up a hot meal from the rear. Their gunners seemed more accurate than ours, and it was extremely foolish to take any chances with them. Those who did usually did not live to tell the tale.

Not all our casualties were caused directly by the Germans. In D Company we had a Corporal Davis and also a Lance-Corporal Davis who, though unrelated, both came from Devon. One day a cow, hit by shell splinters and running away in panic, fell on top of Corporal Davis in his slit trench. Almost incredibly, exactly the same accident happened next day to Lance-Corporal Davis. Each of them had a broken leg, and they were evacuated to England. When I returned to the company after my convalescence, I was amused and rather chagrined to find both wearing wound stripes. However, the origin was not forgotten as they were always known as "The Cow Trod-ons".

Whenever the opportunity arose, we retrieved Luger and Walther automatic pistols from dead Germans and compared them with our own Brownings. We used to see how quick we were on the draw and how fast we could take aim. One day two good friends, Corporal Dick "Blanco" White and Jimmy Birch were engaged in an amicable contest. Blanco's pistol went off and Jimmy Birch dropped dead, shot through the heart. Blanco was reduced to the ranks, but that did not worry him as he never really overcame his grief at having killed his best friend. When on leave he had the courage to visit Jimmy Birch's parents to tell them how their son had died, and I do not suppose it was a matter of any great regret to him when he was killed at the Rhine crossing.

Despite all the action and the loss of so many friends, the war still seemed unreal to me. It was all so much like live ammunition exercises in England.

Always it was the other man who got killed or wounded, and there was still time for jokes and banter.

The most nerve-racking hours were the nights, fortunately short in June. As we were in a defensive position, we had no need to send out patrols to discover where the enemy were, but every night German patrols were out, feeling for our positions. To hear a German patrol only twenty yards away at night, moving through the rustling grass and young corn, was a nerve-tingling experience. We strained our eyes and ears to the limit, but we never gave away our positions by opening fire. However, we sadly missed our poacher, Joe Boston, as he had always been at home in the dark. He seemed to know just where the enemy were and would hop from slit trench to slit trench with scarcely a sound, whispering encouragement to his men. At the end of each nerve-racking night we greeted the dawn with heartfelt gratitude. We had survived to see the sun again. That was how we lived — on a day-to-day basis only.

D-Day-plus-four dawned dull and sombre as Flannelfoot Guthrie returned from a briefing at Company HQ with the news that D Company would be relieved. Not a matter for congratulating ourselves, as we were only to be transferred to the centre of the bridgehead, where a major German attack was expected. To make matters worse, flying conditions were bad, so if any assault did come, we could expect no air support, and even before being relieved we were to learn the difference between ground fighting with and without air superiority.

The first wave of planes appeared just after stand-to at about 5a.m. They were Messerschmitt 109s, something like our Spitfires but with almost rectangular wings. Their underside was painted entirely black, save for white crosses on the wings, presumably so that they would not show up in the searchlights at night, but the effect was decidedly sinister and fearsome. They were armed with machine-guns and cannon for strafing ground troops, which, for the next few hours, meant us, and in our fortified farmyard it seemed that the whole Luftwaffe was intent on a personal vendetta. We hit back as best we could. The fire from the Bofors was almost continuous; Joe French was busy with the Bren-gun, while I blazed away with my rifle. Goodness knows what the odds must be against bringing down a plane attacking at tree-top height at over 300 m.p.h. Still it kept up morale better to have a go than just lying at the bottom of our slit trenches, doing nothing. As it happened, our platoon lost no men, thanks to being well dug in, but the Bofors crew, with less cover, suffered two casualties.

As abruptly as the aerial attack began, so it ended. One minute enemy planes seemed to be everywhere; then there were none. Sergeant Walters waited for ten seconds or so and then ordered me up to the look-out post in the roof of a barn. "Stay there until I say come down," he ordered. On this occasion I did not obey and must have broken the record for the fastest descent from that vulnerable position.

Less than five minutes after the ME109s disappeared, I spotted, high in the sky, a flight of

Focke-Wolfe 190s. These, I knew, were dive bombers. They were, in fact, dive-bombers-cum-single-engined fighters, like the American Thunderbolts. They were painted black on the underside, but I could see racks of small bombs under each wing, as they dived at about 400 m.p.h. Within seconds bombs were exploding all around the farmyard. The roof of the barn received a direct hit, and some of the tiles fell around me as I hurtled through the air, to land, half-winded, on some sacks of grain about twelve feet below. I had enough breath left to pick myself up and dash for the cover of my slit trench, where I kept my head well down till the raid was over. The experience was rather surprising. It had begun and ended so quickly that I had not had time to feel afraid. It must have been quite a near thing, though, because, when I put my head up and gave the thumbs-up sign to Bert Walters in the next slit trench, he looked quite relieved.

We had to put up with this sort of harassment all that June morning. Looking back, after the ordeal was over, I had every sympathy with those other soldiers in other armies who had faced the Panzers backed up by the Luftwaffe. I could appreciate how the Poles in 1939, the BEF and French, Dutch and Belgians in 1940 and the Russians in 1941 must have felt when the *Blitzkrieg* was launched against them. Personal gallantry with rifles and bayonets is no sort of answer to this type of warfare.

Not only were we rather worried for our own sakes by this sustained attack, but Flannelfoot Guthrie and Sergeant Walters were obviously increasingly anxious about the ability of the relief troops to get through to us, so that we in turn could go to the support of the centre section. However, about midday, between air raids, infantrymen of the 51st Highland Division eventually turned up, and one of their platoons took over our half-demolished farmyard. Now that it was time to leave, we felt quite sad at quitting what had been our home ever since D-Day. It had not been a comfortable home, but it was here that we had received our baptism of fire and, as we crept out, I breathed a prayer of gratitude that I was still alive.

As we in D Company had been four days in action, we were put in reserve about a mile behind the front line, and most of us had the first decent sleep since embarking on board the LCTs. Long before morning, however, the increasing din woke us, and when we stood to at first light, the German assault had already started.

It began as usual with a mortar barrage; then the infantry attacked, supported by tanks. Once again, the Luftwaffe were out in strength, but this time they were not having it all their own way. The weather had improved, and all day long the aerial battles raged overhead, with neither side gaining an overwhelming advantage. We watched the dog-fights with fascination and concluded that, after all, we on the ground were going to have to win this war. Suddenly we heard a roar that sounded for all the world like a tube train thundering overhead. Seconds later an almighty explosion occurred a mile or so away. We were quite at a loss to know what was going on until Flannelfoot explained that the Navy was joining in. What we were hearing were the one-ton shells for the sixteen-inch guns of the battleship *Rodney* passing overhead. "Thank God the Navy are with us," I thought, and hoped that the gunners would not lower their sights and send a shell our way.

All day long we waited for orders, but none came, and the only relief from the boredom of inaction was the sight of small groups of prisoners who, from midday onwards, passed us *en route* to the POW cages at the rear. They walked with hands on their heads, prodded by the rifles and bayonets of their escorts, and for the first time I realized what being a prisoner of war meant — a humiliation that I was to experience later on. The first that came my way I waved on with my rifle and bayonet, to indicate the direction they had to take; then I noticed that they seemed to be bunching into a queue. Walking over, I saw that about half a dozen of the regular pre-war soldiers, including NCOs from both D Company and the companies from up front, were searching the prisoners — but not for weapons. Watches, rings, money and anything of any value were all being stripped from the men. It was fairly obvious that the Germans were expecting it; anyway, they were not protesting. Later on that day I was again to see the same vultures at work.

In the early afternoon, just as we finished our lunch of Jem Hacker's usual delicious stew, followed by "Burma Road" (boiled rice with raisins) and a mug of "gunfire" (hot, steaming, sweet tea), the order came. "Stand to. Prepare to move."

We gathered that there had been a German break-through and that our task was to go and drive them out of the village of Breville and plug the gap. As it was on a narrow front, the Company Commander decided to attack with two platoons abreast and the other two platoons following up. Mine was in the second wave, for which I was profoundly thankful. After some bitter fighting the enemy were pushed back, and a number of them surrendered, when my platoon was detailed to escort the prisoners to the rear, where once again I saw the poor devils being robbed of all their valuables by the same old soldiers.

What sickened me more than anything was the sight of one NCO, a veteran of the North-West Frontier, taking watches and rings from the dead. When a ring was too tight, he promptly drew his dagger and stripped off the flesh, leaving just the skeleton finger-bone. Then, cleaning the flesh off, he would pocket the ring. Another of the vultures I saw actually robbing the bodies of false teeth and gold fillings. I did not consider myself squeamish and thought I was becoming hardened to war and killing, but I had to turn away before I was sick. At the end of the war we heard the stories of Belsen and other German concentration camps, and there was much horror and indignation that men and women could do such things. But I knew that, had there been concentration camps in Britain, there would have been no shortage of volunteers to staff them. I had seen some of them at work.

A few hours later it was not "the other man" who got wounded, and I started my journey back to England with which I opened this narrative.

CHAPTER
NINE

Hospital and Home

The journey in the hospital train from Portsmouth lasted only a few hours, but by this time I was extremely uncomfortable. My leg was hurting badly, and I had not had a morphia jab for several hours. Also my behind was as sore as a gumboil from all those blunt needles, and I could not lie on my side even if I had wanted to, for there I was still tightly strapped to the stretcher. But there was a bright side. At least I was on dry land, out of earshot of guns and planes, and proper medical attention could not be far away. Moreover, the sun was shining.

Journey's end was a hospital in Chichester, where two very attractive nurses took charge of me. They stripped off all my clothes, gave me a blanket bath and tucked me in bed in a pair of crisp, clean pyjamas. I was far too tired to make any protest or even to feel self-conscious. They also gave me a complete toilet set, so I was able to indulge in the luxury of cleaning my teeth, for the first time for days; and then an orderly using a brand-new razor gave me a shave. I remember thinking that it was strange that such ordinary things, which we usually take for granted, change into luxuries when we are deprived of them.

No sooner was I tucked up in bed than a doctor arrived to pull back the bedclothes and examine me. He removed the field dressing, examined the wound and gave orders to a couple of orderlies who were hovering in the background. Once more I found myself on a stretcher. For forty-eight hours I had been lying on the stretcher where I was dumped in Normandy, and now here I was, back on another one. This time, though, I was mounted on wheels and on my way to the operating theatre. A nurse gave me a jab in the arm — just to soothe me, she explained — but then produced what seemed to me an enormous syringe with which she proceeded to inject something into the vein in the crook of my arm. The trolley attendants meantime had been chaffing me.

"Where do you live?" one asked.

I told him, Walthamstow.

"Tough guys, you blokes from Walthamstow," he was saying as black oblivion closed around me.

I woke at about ten o'clock the next morning. Bright sunlight was pouring through a window and shining on my white bed and on two nurses who were standing looking at me. I tried to move but found it impossible. Not only was I bandaged from hip to knee but two weighted pillows were fastened to either side. I was anchored as securely as if I had been in a strait-jacket.

The nurses fed me with tea, from a feeder of all things, and a soft-boiled egg. The bread and butter was cut in slices, with the crusts removed. What luxury, what pampering. I thoroughly relished it, especially as I had had no food for almost seventy-two hours.

Feeling a little livelier after that repast, I asked the nurses why I was trussed up like a stuffed fowl. The doctor would be along in a minute, they said, and he would explain everything; they were not allowed to discuss my wounds with me. Wounds, I thought. They must mean "wound". I don't have more than one. But they were right. When the doctor turned up, he told me that, when they had me in the operating theatre, they had given me a thorough examination and found that there was another wound that had previously been over-looked.

"Nothing to worry about though," said the doctor. "You have a small piece of shrapnel embedded in the middle of the muscle of your right thigh. We tried to dig it out, but it would have caused so much damage that we decided to leave it in. It may stay there for the rest of your life, or it may slowly work itself out."

"Slowly" was the operative word. Nearly forty years later the shell splinter is still there and has not even started to work its way to the surface. I guess I must accept that it is now part of me.

The doctor also told me that the main reason for my being so tightly strapped was that I was to be moved that day to a hospital in the north of England. "You'll be safer there," he said. So off I went, on yet another stretcher. However, I was beginning to take pleasure in possessions again and had my new toilet gear and a dressing-gown, as well as my watch, money and Army pay book. I also kept, for sentimental reasons, my Army battledress with all the Airborne insignia on it, and my old flying-smock which was charred and ragged where the shrapnel passed through on its way to the flesh beneath. It was good to see all these things again and to check that nothing was missing. In particular I was glad to have my red beret, which I had worn on the stretcher, ever since I discarded my steel helmet in Normandy. No Red Devil would ever willingly part with that, I thought as I smiled to myself. I knew all along that I was going to survive — I *had* to survive, for I was, after all, a member of a *corps d'élite*. I was a Red Devil.

The doctor and the two nurses came to see me off.

"You're lucky you didn't get the DSO," laughed the doctor, as I was being wheeled out.

"That's only awarded to commissioned officers, not lance-corporals," I told him.

"What I mean is," said the doctor grinning, "that seeing where your wound is, you're lucky you didn't get your dick shot off."

I felt myself bushing as I was wheeled away by the laughing orderlies, to the background of giggling from the two pretty nurses.

Once more into an ambulance and once more on board a hospital train, but this time I was much more comfortable. A number of RAMC orderlies travelled with us, and we had all been given food packs, fruit, cigarettes and other goodies. At each stop our train was met by kind middle-aged ladies who fed us with bars of chocolate and cups of tea and who gave us kisses like mothers welcoming their sons home. It was really touching. We were in good spirits, swopping jokes and yarns and relating how we had been wounded. Most of us had wounds that would heal, given time, though one poor devil in our carriage had lost a leg and refused to be cheered up no matter how hard we tried. However, he did not complain, and his quiet courage left me with a feeling of humility and gratitude that I had got off as lightly as I had.

The journey was less prolonged and arduous than might have been expected as usually the railways during the war did not function at maximum efficiency. Once on a train, one could never be sure where it would go or how many changes would be necessary before the proper destination was reached. Every serviceman in the country must have spent many hours waiting at Crewe Station. Indeed, we used to reckon that a man was not properly qualified as a member of HM Forces until he had put in his stint on one of the Crewe platforms — it was like registering for National Service or passing one's medical, so we were decidedly surprised when, having skirted London, we went through Crewe without even stopping.

I was asleep when the train drew in at Ormskirk, a small, friendly Lancashire town, and was awakened by the sound of carriage doors opening and of blunt northern accents. Getting us all unloaded was a lengthy proceeding as there were several hundred stretcher cases and only about half a dozen ambulances, each taking only four stretchers at a time to a hospital a mile or two away. However, all things eventually come to an end, and by eight o'clock that evening, several hours after the train had stopped, I found myself finally tucked into bed by a nurse. Thank God, I thought, now I can settle down at last.

Not ten seconds later I was on the move again. Where now? I thought wearily. But it was only to another part of the ward. The porter wheeling me said that one of the other patients had seen me brought in and had asked for my bed to be moved alongside. It was Joe French! If I had been able, I would have jumped out of bed and hugged him. The last time we had been together we had been lying four feet apart in a slit trench, after the mortar bomb had landed between us. Now here we were again, lying four feet apart, with a blonde bombshell standing between us, and once again we could not do a darned thing about it.

Passing the time for the next two months or so while we were confined to bed promised to be a problem, especially in view of the active life we were used to. We started off by playing chess. Joe taught me the game, and we were soon playing for hours on end. Then we began to take it too seriously and to argue about it, so we stopped before we fell out.

We were so far from our homes that neither of us had any family visitors; nor, for that matter, did many of the other men. We quite understood that everyone was busy at war work and that, anyway, travelling was very difficult. But the kindness of the Lancashire people more than made up for the absence of relations. The townsfolk of Ormskirk really took us to their hearts. We were made to feel so welcome that Joe and I agreed it was just like home, only better. In one respect, we had an advantage. Our wards were two wooden huts built as an extension of the main hospital, just inside the compound gates. So people could pop in and out easily. Girls would come in with flowers; elderly ladies dropped in to read to us and to write letters for those men who were unable to use their hands. One dear old lady used to look in just for a moment once a week to give Joe her weekly ration of one egg.

When we were able to move about and go into the town, the men were just as kind. None of us who managed to struggle into one of the pubs ever had to buy his own drink. They were truly great and wonderful people, those citizens of Ormskirk.

Sometimes, thirty odd years on, as I look back on those war-time days, the realization of what we have lost saddens me. Only those of us who lived through them can appreciate how united we were and how willingly we helped one another through the troubles. If only we could recapture that same spirit, with someone as great a leader as Winston Churchill, even now we could be the happiest and most prosperous nation on earth.

Back now to the blonde beauty whom we found standing between us on our first evening at the hospital. She proved to be Audrey, the matron's niece. She was in the WRNS, and a very pretty Wren she was too, with just enough puppy fat left to make her nice and cuddly. The matron, however, was a right old battleaxe. All the patients and nursing staff and even some of the doctors went in fear of her, so I thought it would not be a bad thing to get on good terms with her niece. In fact, we became very good friends.

Audrey seemed to get plenty of leave. She had been posted to the Lancashire coast, near Southport — a place so near the hospital that even when on duty she could usually come over to visit her aunt most evenings. At least, she ostensibly came to visit her aunt, but I think I saw more of her than her aunt did. She would wheel me down town in a wheelchair to a servicemen's club, opened by a church organization for the benefit of us wounded. She also used to creep into the ward after lights out for a kiss and cuddle. That was as far as our romance progressed though. I never could figure out whether she was really virtuous or whether she had not fallen for me after all, but was only being considerate on account of my having been wounded. I was never to find out, for by the time I was on my feet again she had been posted to another part of the country, and we never met again.

The matron was not the only battleaxe in the hospital. The Irish day sister, Sister Murphy, was just about as bad. The doctors were reasonably easy-going with us and allowed us to get up and move around if we felt like it, or even go down town, but Sister Murphy was altogether a different proposition. She was a real martinet who enjoyed showing her authority, as when she insisted on our using bed-pans even when we were able to hobble along to the toilet — an order which we found humiliating.

I could see it was going to be a long time before I got down town, if I had to rely on Sister Murphy's permission, and down town was where I had been itching to go for weeks. But Red Devils are not easily thwarted by nursing sisters, and as soon as I felt I was able to make the expedition, Joe French and I devised a plan for outwitting her.

One day we waited till she had gone off to lunch, and then Joe helped me to walk round to the stores and pick up trousers, socks, shirt, boots, underwear and other accessories, including a walking-stick. We had it safely stowed in my locker and I was back in bed about five minutes before she returned for her afternoon round. Next day, again during her lunch hour, Joe and I got dressed and went off down town. We looked around for a time — it was great to be back in the outside world again — then sat down in the servicemen's club for an hour or two, enjoying tea and cakes, before returning to the hospital. As expected, Sister Murphy was waiting for us. She gave us the mother and father of a rollicking, using language which she had not picked up at her daily Mass. We waited for the storm to blow over, and when she came to change my dressing, she could see that I was none the worse for my outing. However, though it could not be said that she softened or relented, she never again tried to prevent us from going out.

Lancashire is, of course, celebrated for its pretty lasses, and Ormskirk was well up to the general standard. We did well in the fortnight that remained before we were to be sent to a convalescent camp. In fact, we had a grand old time. We went for walks in the woods and enjoyed afternoon tea dances on early closing days. In the evening we had free access to pubs and pictures. We even managed to persuade a couple of girls to take time off from work to go to Southport two or three times, on the pretext that we thought the sea air would do us good. Unfortunately for that argument, we never seemed to get farther than the sand-dunes, but apparently they did not notice. All great fun but unappreciated by Sister Murphy, who expressed disappointment at my rate of recovery, which seemed to have slowed down, requiring four weeks, instead of two, before I was fit to be transferred to the convalescent camp. She acidly commented that I would do better to stay in the ward in the evening, participating in the singsongs, beetle and whist drives organized for us by kindly and patriotic ladies. I did not contradict her.

But all good things come to an end, and eventually I was put on the transfer list. I never saw or heard of any of the girls again, but I left them in full confidence that they would continue to do their best for the country's war effort in general and its wounded soldiers in particular.

Joe and I were discharged from hospital in the middle of August 1944 and sent to Trentham Gardens Convalescent Camp, on the outskirts of Stoke-on-Trent, where the whole emphasis was on building up our physical fitness, but discipline was not harsh, and it was a splendid place to be in. The surroundings were beautiful, the training was easy, and there were plenty of girls. Unfortunately there was one big problem. We were allowed to draw only 2 shillings a day of our pay, the rest being credited to our Army pay account.

Although the cost of living was much lower in 1944 than it is today, on our first Friday pay parade Joe and I looked with disdain at our meagre pittance of 14 shillings and wondered how on earth we were going to make it last through the week.

Our first call was to the NAAFI, to buy our tax-free cigarettes, and as neither of us smoked more than ten a day, 4 shillings' worth were enough to see us through till next pay day. That left 10 shillings for other expenses.

In the evening we went out to get a drink at the "Bunch of Grapes", a pub recommended to us by the other lads at the convalescent camp. It was a big, fairly modern place with a swinging sign depicting a lady in a loosely fitting Grecian gown, holding up a bunch of black grapes and displaying one bare bosom. Known throughout the camp as "The Swinging Tit", it was reckoned to be the best in town, so with beer at a shilling a pint and 10 shillings each to spend, we devoted the evening to consuming ten pints. However, this left us penniless to face the rest of the week. On the Saturday Joe and I went to the town in the afternoon without a bean in our pockets. Walking through the shopping area, we met a couple of girls and started chatting them up, but when it came to discussing what we should do that evening, I had to tell mine that, much as I would have liked to take her to the pictures, I had no money. She immediately offered to pay for us both. At first I naturally refused, but, after a convincing token resistance, I gave in, and Joe did the same, so that was how we contrived to enjoy a reasonably good social life on 14 shillings a week.

The girls enjoyed it as much as we did, but I was a little disconcerted when, about two nights before we were due to leave the camp, mine brought the conversation round to love and marriage. Back at camp, I mentioned this to Joe and learned that his had given him the same treatment and that some of the others had had similar experiences, so on our last night at Trentham Gardens we had an all male farewell party, since, pleasant though things were, a permanent relationship was the last thing we wanted, let alone marriage.

From the convalescent camp Joe and I were sent home on ten days' leave, Joe to Somerset and myself to London. My family had by now returned to their old home, and my father was engaged in repairing the damage being done by the V1 flying bombs, so it was back to sleeping in the air-raid shelter. I enjoyed being with my family again but, as all my old school friends were away in the Services and I was missing the comradeship of the Army, I soon became bored. Every time I wandered into a pub, somebody was sure to ask, though quite kindly, "When are you going back?" When my ten days' leave was up, I was quite glad to go.

Reporting back to Oxford, I met Joe again. We were given a medical inspection, passed as fit and sent to a staging camp at Aldershot, from which reinforcements were being sent to Normandy, but, as the only Red Devils in the camp, we were not on any list, and nobody seemed to know what to do with us. Every morning on parade we made certain of avoiding any unpleasant tasks by standing in the rear rank when men were being detailed for duties in the cookhouse or latrines and for other fatigues. The parade over, we would fall out and spend the rest of the day playing snooker and darts at the YMCA, returning to camp only for lunch and for the evening meal.

The other young chaps in our hut thought we were a couple of real old veterans and were forever asking us what it was like in action, how did we get wounded, how much did it hurt and so on. We began to feel battle-scarred warriors of infinite experience. It sooned palled though, and after a couple of weeks we grew tired of the inactivity. All the other men were ordinary infantry, and groups were daily sent to reinforce infantry battalions in Normandy. We supposed that sooner or later our time was bound to come, but we decided that, if we had to go back into action again, we would rather do it with the Red Devils. So one morning we asked for and were granted an interview with the camp Commanding Officer, who was entirely sympathetic. He immediately telephoned our battalion HQ on Salisbury Plain, explaining that he had a couple of their men and asking whether they wanted us. To our relief, the answer was a quick "Yes". Within an hour we had packed our kits, received our travel warrants and were on our way back to our old battalion unit.

CHAPTER
TEN

Father-Figure
— At Nineteen

There was only a skeleton staff at the camp when we arrived, and we immediately felt an atmosphere between the men who had been in action and those who had not. There were men like ourselves who had been wounded and had now found their way back into the battalion, there were the usual maintenance staff, and there were also a few men under arrest and awaiting court martial. The acting commanding officer was a tubby, easy-going but not unpleasant man named Major Percy Pearman who had been a reserve officer with the battalion. He had not been in action and we wondered if the men would have confidence in him should we be sent into action again.

Joe and I were separated and never again went into action together. He was put on general duties while, as a lance-corporal, I joined the guard room staff, to help look after the prisoners. These passed the day cutting the grass on the football pitches with reaping-hooks, while I sat and watched them, nursing a sten-gun and marching them back to the guard room for meals and sleep. I didn't know what their crimes were and didn't want to. Probably cowardice, sleeping on duty while on active service, insubordination or something like that. One or two were really hard cases, and my only concern was that none of them should escape as I did not want to get involved in a court martial myself.

Fortunately this period did not last long as the battalion, which had suffered heavy casualties, was withdrawn from Normandy and sent back to Salisbury Plain in readiness for the time when airborne troops would again be required. Our new battalion commander was Lieutenant-Colonel Charlton, and, to my great disappointment, the new company commander of D Company was Major Pearman. Even worse, our sergeant-major was the unpopular and unlikeable Jem Hacker. There was, however, no time to dwell on such matters. With only a quarter of the original members of D Company still on the strength, the gaps had to be filled by newcomers. I was promoted to the rank of corporal and given charge of ten men, not one of whom had ever been in action. The training programme started all over again, but this time at a greatly accelerated rate, for we were at eight hours' notice to go back to France. Surveying my bunch of rookies, I prayed to God to be allowed two or three months to get them into shape before that occurred.

As it happened, I had just short of three months to make good fighting men out of them. Sometimes I allowed myself a wry smile at the thought that here was I, still under twenty years, though with the rank of corporal and a wound stripe on my arm, being regarded as a kind of father-figure by the young eighteen-year-olds who formed my section. They were just as I was when joining the Red Devils.

I got to know them individually. The riflemen were Cecil or Cyril Jakoff, Frank Ponsonby, a boy named Gibson, Joe Mullins, Jack Nichols and Ted Lockey. No one was ever quite sure of Jakoff's first name, and anyhow with a label like Jakoff he was promptly dubbed Jak. He was a small, dark boy of Russian-Jewish descent, and his looks advertised his ancestry. He was only about five foot two and had to put up with a lot of ragging because of his size, but he could take it. A Londoner, he was as chirpy as a sparrow, had a marvellous sense of humour and a gift of quick repartee and was a real asset to the section.

His mate in the section, with whom he would have to share a slit trench, was Frank Ponsonby, a tall, dark, well-built and good-looking public schoolboy from the wealthy zone of Cheshire where the rich businessmen of Manchester live. He could have gone to university and stayed out of the Army much longer, but he defied his family to join up. He and Jak made a good pair, far and away more intelligent than the Army average but able to fit in with the team.

Gibson also came from a good family and was evidently pleased with the chance to escape from them for a time. He too was a tall boy, with brown, wavy hair, and he quickly achieved the reputation of being the section's ladies' man. Doubtless he found Army life less restricting than life at home in this respect. Jak promptly christened him "Tombstone" on account of one false tooth in his upper set, which he would continually take out and replace at times of stress.

Joe Mullins was another cockney — a big, strong man who obeyed every order without hesitation and was a very reliable soldier. Jack Nichols, yet another cockney, who had worked in the London docks, was tall, with dark, wavy hair and a pencil-slim moustache. He had both the appearance and the instincts of a first-class spiv, but he was a good soldier, did as he was told and kept out of trouble.

Ted Lockey had a quite remarkable physique. Only about 5½ feet tall, he was almost as broad. He was immensely powerful. I remember seeing him carrying the ball in a game of Shrove Tuesday football. There seemed to be about six men on his back, but he was charging ahead like a tank, and it was only when someone dived at his feet and grabbed his legs that he went down.

The Bren-gunner was Alfie Ross, a powerful man of medium height from Exeter. In civvy street he worked for the roads department of the local council, operating a "Stop and Go" board at roadwork sites, which he seemed to think was such a responsible job that it ought to have kept him out of the Army. He was obviously not blessed with a surfeit of brains but did as he was told. No. 2 on the bren-gun was Ray Best, another Devonshire lad, who was likewise malleable and willing. I reckoned it was best to keep the two West Country men together. Incidentally, with the re-formation of D Company, the former West Country preponderance had disappeared. Most of the new men were from the South, the Midlands or London.

Because all the men in my section were newcomers, I needed a second-in-command as lance-corporal who had had some experience. So I was able to persuade the sergeant to let me have one of the Normandy survivors, Harry Harris, in whom I came to have absolute confidence. A tall, thin Wessex lad, Harry had been wounded in Normandy and torpedoed on the way back to England but had returned to the Red Devils as soon as he was fit.

31 Platoon was, of course, still in D Company, and our new platoon sergeant was Charlie Ashton, the six-foot cockney I had last seen on the LST bringing us back from Normandy. He was a bit too tall for his safety, his height making him conspicuous in action. There were many times when I was glad that I was of medium height. He was a quiet, well-mannered man who rarely found it necessary to raise his voice, but he always got his own way, and the men pulled their weight for him. As long as they did, he was easy to get on with.

Our platoon commander, Lieutenant Bill Collins, arrived among us in a typically dramatic style. One day when we were training on the plain a light aircraft landed not far away and came taxi-ing across to us. Out jumped a man in Airborne uniform with two pips on his shoulder.

"Hey!" he shouted. "Can any of you guys tell me how to get to this unit?"

When we had properly identified him, we told him he had arrived.

Bill Collins was a Canadian. Slightly above medium height and broadly built, with a thatch of straw-coloured hair, he had a decidedly boyish look to his freckled face. His presence was like a breath of fresh air. In camp he naturally lived and messed in the officers' quarters, but on exercises he always ate with the men, and if there was an opportunity of having a drink with the lads, he would always take it, insisting that he stood his round first.

I remember a night on Dartmoor, when we were engaged on an exercise using live ammunition. Some of the men decided they would go down to Okehampton when off duty, and one bright spark there suggested that gin and rough cider (scrumpy) would make a good drink. Only Bill Collins stuck to his Scotch. When we finally emerged from the pub at about half-past ten, it was soon obvious that we had not a hope of getting back to camp in time. The route was some two or three miles, up a hill with a one-in-six gradient, and in our state of happy euphoria we were hardly capable of walking straight on the level, let alone climbing steep hills. Bill Collins, however, was equal to the emergency. Spotting a fifteen-hundred-weight truck driven by a corporal of the transport platoon, he stopped it by displaying his rank and then ordered the driver to take us all back to camp. Turfing out the corporal's mate, he took the front seat next to the corporal. About ten men scrambled into the back, while another six rode on the canvas roof. Thus laden, the truck struggled manfully up the hills. A hundred yards from camp, he stopped the truck, ordered the men out and told us to proceed to camp quietly. And woe betide us if we did not put on a bloody good show on parade the next morning!

Training started slowly but soon gained momentum, and my motto was: "If there's going to be a passenger in this section, it'll be me; the rest of you will do what you're told." They accepted this philosophy without argument. There was, of course, a distinct advantage in the fact that this new intake of recruits was being trained by men with battle experience since their knowledge gave an added edge to the routine of weapon-training, flying, battle-drill, exercise and route marches.

One of our companies had carried out a forced march in battle order, towing handcarts, around a course of 17½ miles in just over four hours. Bets had been laid all round the officers' mess that this time could not be beaten, so of course every company had a try — some had two or three. Eventually D Company beat the record, with a time of three hours and forty-five minutes, during which marathon three men dropped out but were picked up and carried along on the handcrafts. Major Pearman was absolutely delighted. He did his best, as he thought it, to encourage us, by driving in his jeep up and down the column for the whole of the 17½ miles.

As the Allied forces were approaching the Rhine, the military authorities decided that what the Red Devils needed before our next embarkation, which would probably be to Germany itself, was a course in street fighting. The Battle of Monte Cassino, in Italy, had shown how difficult it was to dislodge a determined

100

enemy from a pile of rubble, so if the Germans were to defend their Fatherland in the towns, street by street and house by house, it was absolutely essential that the assault troops received sufficient training in this comparatively new type of warfare. The battalion was therefore sent to a bombed area of Birmingham for two weeks to gain some experience.

The culmination of the fortnight was an inter-company competition over a street-fighting assault course of about two miles. It involved tunnelling under houses, searching the whole street house by house, balancing along parapets and finally jumping off a roof. A lot of teamwork was needed to get round the course in good time, defusing mines, booby traps and other devices on the way. On this occasion D Company failed miserably, our time for the course being the worst of all by a considerable margin. Major Pearman probably lost all the wager money he had raked in on his bets over the forced marches. We felt sure that he had given Jem Hacker a hell of a rocket, for training and discipline was in the hands of the NCOs, and the sergeant-major of the company was ultimately responsible.

It could not be expected that Jem Hacker would keep his troubles to himself, and with every intention of passing on the wigging he had received, he stormed around D Company's lines, looking for victims. When he burst into 31 Platoon's hut, most of the men were lying on their beds, reading, but four or five others and myself were playing pontoon for small stakes.

Gambling is, of course, banned in the Army, but in order to press home a charge it is necessary for the prosecuting officer or NCO to produce not only the pack of cards but the money involved. As the door burst open, the money miraculously disappeared. Into whose pockets did not matter; all that concerned us was that no money was to be seen. Blustering in, Jem Hacker picked on me as usual — for some reason he always seemed to have it in for me and take every advantage of his higher rank to make my life uncomfortable. Anyway, that's the way it seemed to me.

Even though the men were supposed to be off duty, he yelled that, as they had done so badly on the street-fighting course, the NCOs ought to have had them all out, training. I did not reply, and he continued ranting and roaring. I still held my tongue. It was a difficult situation. If I had replied, I could have been accused of defying a warrant officer; if I remained silent, I could be accused of dumb insolence.

"You're on a charge before the Company Commander, nine o'clock tomorrow morning, Corporal," he shouted in conclusion, storming out of the hut and slamming the door.

It could be wrong to say I was not worried. I knew I could be demoted to private and lose pay. Still, there was not much I could do about it.

At 09.00 hours next morning I was marched in before Major Pearman and told I was in serious trouble. The sergeant-major was accusing me of neglect of duty, insolence to a warrant officer and gambling.

I answered the neglect of duty charge by saying that my section was around average for the company. In the circumstances, with only two experienced soldiers in the section, I thought they had done reasonably well. It had not entered my mind, I said, to take the men out for special training afterwards, though if some of the other NCOs had taken the lead, I was sure I would have followed suit. I also denied being insolent to the sergeant-major. He had made it clear that we had done badly and, in the circumstances I could not disagree, especially in front of the men, so I had thought it best to say nothing. Major Pearman then asked about the gambling charge and said that, as there was no evidence, he would decide the matter on my word.

"Now, Corporal," he said formally, "were you or were you not gambling?"

"No, sir," I lied, smartly.

He then pronounced judgement.

"Case dismissed on all three charges."

Jem Hacker did not look at all pleased.

Before I could be marched out, Major Pearman reminded me that next day was the battalion cross-country championship run. He hoped that D Company would do well and said that, as one of their best runners, I was expected to put up a good performance. Talking to me like a Dutch uncle, he urged me to put the recent unfortunate business behind me. I was now one of the more experienced NCOs in the company, he continued, and the newer men would be looking to me for leadership.

"Very good, sir," I said and saluted smartly.

It was clear that he recognized that he needed men like me in his company and also that he realized, from the weakness of the evidence, that there was some friction between Jem Hacker and myself. As for Hacker, he never again tried to nail me officially. It began to look as if I was one of Percy's blue-eyed boys, and he did not want to run into trouble with him. However, he got his own back a few days later in a game of football. He was a first-rate footballer, hard as granite, and could have made the grade as a professional if he had not been a regular soldier. On this occasion he launched what appeared to be a simple tackle against me from behind, but the result was that I finished up with two badly bruised ankles which had me hobbling for several days. I accepted the situation without complaint as I knew I could not win all the time.

Following my dismissal from the charges, I had to attend a team meeting of the best dozen or so runners in the company. There were to be between nine hundred and a thousand runners in the event, of whom about a hundred and thirty would be from D Company, but Sergeant Dixie Howard, who was in charge of our team, had decided to brief only the top dozen or so in his tactical talk, since only the first ten men home in each company would count in the team placings. The top three runners (and I was reckoned as number three) were to act independently and make their own way round the course, while the rest were to run in groups as near the front as possible, taking turns to lead and therefore sharing the burden of pacemaking.

As it turned out, at the end of the seven-mile run I finished eighth in the whole field — the first man home for D Company, which won the team event and Major Pearman his bets. Everybody was happy, except Jem

Hacker, and I was selected for the Divisional Cross-Country Championships, which gave the major some pleasure.

This also brought me a bonus as I was allowed time off from general training to prepare, and on the day before the big race my fellow competitors and I were excused all duties. We spent some time walking around the course, then went down to Salisbury for the evening. On returning to camp just before midnight, the Sergeant of the Guard ordered us to report immediately to our action stations. I ran to 31 Platoon hut and saw all the men packed and ready to leave. The division was leaving Salisbury Plain that night, Sergeant Ashton explained to me, on Montgomery's explicit instructions, to join in what was later to be known as the Battle of the Bulge or, more officially, the Ardennes Offensive.

CHAPTER
ELEVEN

Christmas in the Bulge

I next learned from Charlie Ashton that this was to be a land and sea operation, not airborne at all. Our company would take three jeeps, each with two trailers. As I was one of the few NCOs in the company with an Army driving licence, I would be travelling with the company transport section as co-driver with Pat Tomkins. Pat was the man who had helped to carry my stretcher out of the first-aid post in Normandy, just over six months earlier.

In less than an hour I was packed and ready to go, but just before the convoy moved off, Major Pearman came to give us a look over and called to Pat and myself to go to Company HQ with him, as he had a special assignment for us. This was to carry two crates of booze in the trailer with all the other gear, to keep him warm when we got to the Ardennes, as the newspapers were reporting heavy snow. It was now 18th December and far from ideal weather for travelling several hundred miles into battle in an open jeep.

The briefing we received was that the Germans, under cover of fog, sleet and snow, had mounted a counter-offensive against the American 1st Army in the

Ardennes, a hilly region in the south-east of Belgium, near the French and Luxembourg frontiers. The attack had met with initial success, overrunning the American Army, and it was expected that the enemy's next objectives were the bridges over the River Meuse at Namur and Dinant. After that they would probably head for Brussels and then on to the coast at Antwerp. Montgomery's 21st Army Group had captured that great port virtually intact and by so doing had drastically cut the length of their supply lines. If Antwerp were to be retaken, not only would these lines be cut but a wedge would be driven between the Allied Armies. It could add another year to the war, allowing Hitler the opportunity to use more of the advanced weapons the Germans had developed and also give a breathing-space to the hard-pressed German war industry.

It was pointed out to us, though, that this was a gambler's last throw. Check it, we were told, and Hitler was beaten. The offensive had been very cleverly conceived. Patrols dressed in American uniforms and speaking good English, presumably with American accents, had infiltrated the American lines and had captured key bridges and road junctions. They had been followed up by massed Panzers, supported by motorized infantry. Virtually the whole of the German Strategic Tank Reserve had been committed. The offensive had started under the cover of appalling weather, which had kept the Allied Air Forces grounded, but the Panzers had steamrollered on through fog and snow and had managed to keep close formation by radio rather than by visual contact. Continually by-passing pockets of resistance, they were now hell-bent for the River Meuse.

Eisenhower had reacted by putting Montgomery in command of all the American troops north of the salient. Monty was already in charge of the British and Canadians there, and his immediate response to his new responsibilities was to move some of his forces, including the Guards Armoured Division from Holland, southwards to the head of the salient. At the same time he sent post-haste for the 6th Airborne Division, which by now had been refitted in England and was ready again for action.

The first objective of the division was the town of Dinant, with its vital bridge across the Meuse. The Panzers too were making for that bridge, and the race was going to be a close-run thing. To get an airborne division on the move on unaccustomed wheels was a massive operation, especially as the troops were scattered for miles around Salisbury Plain. It was the early hours of the next morning before our jeep was eventually on its way. The rest of the company had gone on ahead, via Dover, while the transport section was sent to Tilbury.

The next night we spent in bell tents which were erected inside large marquees in a staging camp just outside Tilbury. Early in the morning we embarked for Calais. The crossing took twenty-four hours and was appallingly rough. December gales were raging up the Channel, and for the only time in my life I was seasick. But so was everyone else. While we were waiting to disembark, however, we did get a hot breakfast and were sufficiently recovered to be able to eat it. Which was just as well, for that was the last hot meal we were to get for nearly three days.

Movement by motor convoy is invariably slow, and our progress was no exception. We made less than twenty miles an hour, continually stopping and starting because of the crush of traffic being generated by the German offensive. When we made our rendezvous for lunch, we were told there was nothing to eat until supper-time; needless to say, there was no supper either, at the next rendezvous point, though we were promised a good breakfast next morning. Again, that did not materialize. The only food that came our way was apples and other fruits and chunks of bread handed to us by the civilians who lined the road and cheered the Red Devils on their way to meet the enemy. These French citizens had seen German invaders in 1870, 1914 and 1940, and now they were very much afraid they were going to see them again. The legend of German invincibility had not yet been destroyed, and as we drove through towns and villages, we could see the fear on the faces of the people and could feel the sense of panic and doom. The hated Boche were coming yet again.

On and on went our convoy. The second day was exactly like the first, as far as food was concerned. There just wasn't any. Pat, myself and the other teams lived on the scraps the grateful civilians gave us, and God knows they could ill afford to spare anything. As well as being hungry we were also bitterly cold in our open jeeps and had to change drivers every hour or so. The towns we passed through and the countless British cemeteries reminded us of what we had read and heard about the First World War. We saw St Omer, Ypres, the Menin Gate and Mons. At the crossroads were signposts to places such as Douai, Lille and even Armentières, the home of the famous, or infamous, Mademoiselle. It was hard to believe from the neatness and orderliness of this well-kept farmland and the tidy little towns that thirty years earlier the area had been a sea of mud, intersected by trenches. But it was easy to see that the local people remembered.

By the middle of the third day we could hear the sound of distant gunfire and realized that we must be nearing the battlefield. Again I found myself indulging in a bout of introspection and self-analysis. Where would I be next day? If I were in action again, what sort of fighting would this be? I knew that, having been tested, I would not be a coward, but I was frightened of being wounded again. I hoped I would not be killed. But more than all, I was apprehensive of going to war under conditions for which I and the rest of the unit had received no training and had no knowledge. Our role was the lightning thrust, the short, sharp bursts of combat, but this looked like being a hard, slogging defensive battle.

During the long, cold periods of inaction I found myself thinking of my new recruits who had never before been in action. Were they at the front already, I wondered, and who was leading them? Would we be involved in hand-to-hand fighting — which most of us detested and feared more than anything else? How would the new men face up to such challenges? I could see that Pat's mind was working along the same lines. After all, we had shared the experiences of Normandy and had some idea of what might lie ahead. But we never discussed our thoughts. It was bad enough thinking about it, without letting down our inner defences and talking about it.

As it happened, D Company had arrived at Dinant one day before we did and just as the Germans reached the other side of the river.

Dinant is a long, narrow town strung along both banks of the River Meuse in a very steep valley, almost a ravine. The main part of the town is on the east bank, dominated by the cliff-top citadel. The bridge which joins the two parts is the only one across the Meuse for many miles both to the north and to the south. Hence its importance to both sides. Although the town of Bastogne, where the Americans had been surrounded and were now holding out valiantly, received more newspaper coverage than any other sector in the Battle of the Bulge, it ought not to be forgotten that the outskirts of Dinant were the farthest point west that the Germans reached in their last offensive. It was here that they were finally halted.

On arrival at Dinant we searched for D Company and eventually found them deployed on the cliff overlooking the west bank of the river. They were being held in reserve, ready to counter-attack should the enemy break through and capture the bridge. They had dug for themselves defensive positions in the grounds of a large convent, almost exactly opposite the citadel on the east bank. On reporting, we were briefed by Jem Hacker on the situation, which sounded very grim.

The bridge had been mined and could be blown up at any moment, on the order of the brigadier in charge of the defence of the town. He was the commander of an armoured brigade, and at least half of his tanks were now on the other side of the bridge, fighting side by side with units of the Red Devils. If the bridge was destroyed, the stranded troops had orders to fight to the last round of ammunition and then to try to get back across the river as best they could. The only Germans who had reached the vicinity had been spotted and captured. British tanks were now blocking all entrances into Dinant from the east, but the nearest German tanks were within two miles of the town, and the Allied Air Forces were still grounded by the weather.

As I was about to rejoin my platoon, a message arrived that Major Pearman wanted to see me at once on a very urgent matter. Tired, cold and hungry, I wondered what on earth was up now but I hurried along to his room. When I knocked on the door, entered and saluted, he asked me in a conspiratorial manner to close the door. Then he enquired, "Did you get that booze through, safe and sound?" I was taken aback. To tell the truth, I had forgotten all about the two boxes. "Yes, sir," I said. Saluting, I ran out to catch Pat Tomkins and make sure we still had our precious cargo. We did, and carried them into the company office. "Thank you very much," was the only comment.

Outside, we cursed both ourselves and him. We had been travelling for three days in the freezing cold in an open jeep and had forgotten we had the wherewithal for stomach-warming draughts just behind us. A bad tactical error.

I was very anxious to see how my section had been getting on in my absence, and I soon found 31 Platoon dug in along the front garden of the convent, which was still occupied by the nuns. The men had not made a bad job of their slit trenches, but, as it was still bitterly cold, I kept them working on improvements. Search parties went out to collect rocks, lengths of timber and corrugated iron, and gradually we fortified each slit trench into a miniature pillbox. The exercise not only kept us busy and warm but also gave us better shelter, and within a day our slit trenches had been transformed into quite comfortable dug-outs.

From my own little fort I could see right down into the town at the bottom of the ravine; also the bridge with streams of traffic moving across, and the citadel on the cliff opposite. It was like a Christmas-card picture. There was very little to indicate that the war was only a mile or so away, behind the cliff.

Our duty roster gave the men two hours on, four hours off, and during the off-duty spells there was little to do, so I decided to take Jak and Tombstone (all of us fully armed, of course) off on the prowl, to see what else was going on in the neighbourhood. About half a mile behind the convent we found a tent some twelve feet square, with the door closed and smoke curling from a stove-pipe in the centre of the roof. No one challenged us, so we opened the door and peeped in. Half a dozen American anti-aircraft gunners were sitting around a hot stove, reading magazines. We had failed to spot their gun, sitting in an orchard on the other side of the hedge, but were surprised that no one was on guard. They made us very welcome, gave us hot chocolate and made way for us to share the heat of the stove. It was the first external heat we had felt for many days, and we were duly grateful but could not help thinking, though, that their approach to war was decidedly casual, with the Germans only a few miles away. Nevertheless, they were good neighbours and, as long as we were at the convent, always made us welcome.

After Christmas the weather changed, the sun came out and there was not a cloud in the sky. It lasted for only about three days, but that was enough for the American Lightnings and the RAF Tiffies (Rocket-firing Typhoons) to destroy the bulk of the enemy armour. From our vantage-point we could watch the planes going in over the cliff on the other side of the river. We waited for the explosions, and every now and again a cloud of black smoke confirmed that yet another tank had been hit by the rockets. It cheered us up no end. The more damage that fell on the enemy from the sky, the less there would be for us to do on the ground.

Looking back, I never could remember which day was Christmas Day or what we had for dinner. The days were all the same, one rolled into another. There was certainly no offer from the Germans to come and join us for a drink, a smoke and a session of carol-singing, as happened on the first Christmas of World War I.

CHAPTER
TWELVE

The Battle of Bure

Soon after Christmas we received orders to quit the convent and advance eastwards over the bridge, and on reaching some high ground a few miles further on we were ordered to dig in. We had just finished our slit trenches and were standing around, admiring each other's handiwork, when we came under fire. I heard a dull crump in the distance, followed by a whistling noise.

"Down!" I yelled and dived into my slit trench. The men looked nonplussed, wondering what in the world I was up to. One or two of them even started to shout, "What's up, Corp?" when the shell burst not fifty yards away.

We were being shelled by a German tank with an eighty-eight-millimetre gun, and by the time the second landed, they were all in their trenches, but their baptism of fire could well have been fatal to some of them.

It was so cold on the windswept hillside during the night that one man of B Company actually froze to death, in spite of the fact that, like everyone else, he was wearing string vest, woollen vest, Army shirt, woollen pullover, battledress, flying-smock, a greatcoat and, finally, a snowsuit.

When we were on our two-hour standing patrol, the minutes passed very slowly. It was wearisome and nerve-racking work, made more so by the near-impossibility of doing it properly. Because of our snowsuits we could hardly make out the positions of our neighbours in the adjoining slit trenches, and we knew that the enemy had snowsuits, too. We conversed in the faintest of whispers and stared at the grotesque shapes formed by the snow in nearby hedgerows. The longer we looked, the more it seemed that parts of the hedgerow were moving, and we strained our ears to catch the slightest sound. After about an hour we decided to open our tins of self-heating soup, and that kept us warm for a little while and also helped to pass the time. We drank with our eyes and ears still straining.

Finally, after what seemed an eternity, but in the tradition of the Red Devils five minutes early, we were aware of an almost silent shuffling in the lane behind us. One by one, the men of the relieving section detached themselves from the darkness to take over from us. While I was still whispering to their leader, reporting that there had been no activity whatever during the past two hours, my section had walked twenty or thirty yards down the lane. Suddenly they panicked and ran helter-skelter to the outskirts of the village, two or three hundred yards away. I dared not call after them and walked at a normal pace until I too was overcome by fear. I could not help thinking of how vulnerable I was, alone in hostile country in the dark, and I broke into a run.

When I entered the house where my section and several others were billeted, I caught some sheepish glances from my own men, but I saved my comments until the next time we were on our own. Then I reminded them that, while it was most unlikely that a German patrol would ambush a section of ten men, they could well pick up a solitary straggler and take him back for interrogation. That my section had deserted me, leaving me to this possible fate, was a crime for which I could have put them all on a charge. The next time it happened, if it ever did, someone would get shot for running away in the face of the enemy. I made the point as strongly as I could, for I knew that our chances of survival in the ordeals ahead lay in our sticking together. There must be complete confidence between us, and I felt that this had not yet been achieved.

The longest night has an ending, and at last the new day dawned. Though still intensely cold, it was again bright and sunny. Just the day for air activity. Sure enough, before long we saw the first Allied planes, speeding eastward to attack the enemy tanks.

Our village had long been deserted by its civilian population, and there was no water or electricity. However, a good hot breakfast came up from Company HQ — canned bacon, baked beans, hunks of bread and hot, sweet tea — just what was needed after such a night. Indeed, we felt so well that after breakfast we wandered down to the horse-trough in the village square, broke the two-inch covering of ice and washed, shaved and cleaned our teeth for the first time for about three days. We were on top of the world.

Bill Collins, who had been called to Company HQ, reappeared at about eleven o'clock and called for the platoon sergeant and section leaders, to give out orders. We were to move off at midday, to capture the village of Bure, a few miles along the road. The Air Forces had reported enemy troops, in the village supported by one Tiger tank, but had been unable to knock out the tank with rockets. The supporting infantry were reported to be at about company strength, so our attack would have to be at battalion strength, to give us numerical superiority. We were also to be supported by three American-built Sherman tanks, this again representing the normal superiority required for tackling the much more powerful German tank. Two were armed with the usual seventy-five-millimetre guns, but the other, known as the M10 Tank Destroyer, was fitted with a British seventeen-pounder anti-tank gun, probably the best anti-tank gun of the war. However, it was by no means certain that the giant Tiger tank would not prove more than a match for our three.

The route to Bure proved to be a full day's march. We marched up and down what seemed to be endless hills through snow-covered forests. New picture-postcard scenes unfolded at every corner. And at every corner the enemy might well have been lurking — but fortunately were not.

The Germans were now in full retreat, and we heard rumours that Bastogne had been relieved and that the attacking enemy forces were in danger of being cut off, but that did not stop them putting up a tremendous resistance.

The plan was for two companies to attack on the flanks while D Company went straight up the road into the village, with two Shermans in support. The M10 Tank Destroyer was to move in from the right flank down a narrow track to link up with D Company in the village, while 31 Platoon was to leave the main company, make a detour to join the M10 and escort it into battle.

D Company soon reached the first houses on the outskirts of the village, walking in Indian file along the verges of the road. Everything was very quiet, just the roar of the tank engines and the crunch of men walking on frozen snow. Suddenly the peaceful scene exploded. The air was alive with noise and with machine-gun and rifle bullets. The men dived for whatever cover they could find, some of them battering down the doors of houses to get in.

Returning the German small-arms fire, D Company cautiously moved forward from house to house. The tanks raked every door and window in the houses ahead with machine-gun fire, and if their fire was returned, they pumped in a seventy-five-millimetre shell. As the two Shermans rounded the bend at the bottom of the main street, the Tiger came out of hiding and advanced towards them. It was confident in its own superiority. The commander knew that the seventy-five-millimetre guns could not hurt him, and so he moved in for the kill, seeking to close the range before demolishing the Shermans. However, the leading one saw the danger that same instant and immediately began to reverse around the bend, thus drawing the Tiger farther down the slope of the main street.

Meantime 31 Platoon had been making its way through gardens and back lanes to link up with the M10. We had succeeded in doing this and were now moving towards the centre of the village down a side lane, at right angles to the main street. The Germans were not yet aware of our advance. The engine noise of our M10 was drowned by the much louder roar of the Tiger and by the crackle of small-arms fire. Taking advantage of buildings that lined the lane, we were able to creep forward to within thirty yards of the junction with the main street. The Tiger halted for a moment at that very junction. Its gigantic bulk entirely blocked the end of our narrow lane. But the Germans were not looking our way. They had eyes only for retreating Shermans and the supporting infantrymen. One could imagine the tank commander calculating how best to deliver the knock-out blows.

At thirty yards range the M10 confirmed its reputation as a tank destroyer. Only one shot was needed. It caught the Tiger right on the joint between the turret and the main body of the tank, and the armour-piercing shell must have hit the ammunition store. A tremendous explosion blew the turret clean off, killing all the crew instantly.

Bill Collins ran forward to the corner to make sure that it was the sole enemy armour we had to deal with. We only had the report of the Air Force pilots, and there was the chance that they had not seen everything.

But nothing more was visible and so, completely dwarfed by the ruined Tiger towering above him, he waved us on. Gamely, our little M10 exerted its strength against the side of the wreck and pushed it into the side of the road. Then it turned to advance up the main street, closely followed by the Shermans.

At this, the German resistance rapidly crumbled. As D Company entered each house from the front, the Germans escaping from the rear were picked off, one by one, by the flank companies from their positions on high ground over-looking the village. In one or two houses some of the more fanatical enemy put up a determined resistance and had to be dislodged by grenades. Most of the remainder, however, surrendered. D Company, mopping up, had the distinction of taking the first prisoners of the Battle of the Bulge. Bill Collins, leading his platoon, set up defensive positions on the far outskirts, as a precaution against possible counter-attacks, but these never came.

It had been a highly successful operation, and the battalion duly received the congratulations of the Divisional Commander. By the time it was over, dusk was falling, so we made ourselves as comfortable as we could for the night in the houses of Bure. Patrols took two-hour stints on the village perimeter, but nothing happened during the night. We were all tired but elated at having fought our first battle without casualties.

Thereafter our advance resembled the war in the Pacific, except that instead of hopping from island to island we hopped from village to village. We ignored the harsh, empty uplands and concentrated on the villages, which offered cover both to the enemy and to ourselves. Advancing Indian-file along the snow-covered roads was slow progress, as we had to proceed cautiously even though the Germans were in full retreat and we were no longer in contact with them. Everywhere we saw the havoc caused by the air attacks. Ruined tanks, trucks, half-tracks and every other type of vehicle were scattered around. The Panzers had certainly taken a pasting.

While all this was going on, New Year's Day had come and gone without anyone noticing it. Remembrance would have been futile, anyway, for, apart from the major, no one had the wherewithal to celebrate. As for helping ourselves, looting in a friendly occupied country is an offence meriting a court martial, so there was no breaking into houses or shops.

Shortly after the first week of the New Year we were pulled back into reserve and spent a very pleasant week in the small town of Civet, just inside the French border, where the townsfolk, especially the girls, made us very welcome. After roll-call in the morning, we had the rest of the day to ourselves and, as we were still in the Ardennes Hills, exercised our ingenuity in making toboggans and sleighs for improvised winter sports. We even held competitive toboggan runs. It was good fun, and no limbs were broken, although we had plenty of spills.

In the evenings most of us would sit around a fire, frying pan after pan of potato chips, having scrounged potatoes and cooking-fat from Company HQ; the exception was, of course, Tombstone, who was usually out in the town looking for talent. We washed the chips down with bottles of wine contributed by the local citizens, who were more than thankful to have escaped another German occupation and not to have been involved in the Battle of the Bulge.

It was a happy delightful interlude, but too good to last. On 20th January we were on the move again, to another sector of the front line.

CHAPTER THIRTEEN

The Brussels "Exhibition"

Our new destination was Holland. While the Battle of the Bulge had been occupying our attention, 21st Army Group's advance had been continuing in the north, against stiffening resistance, so we Red Devils were sent to help out. We were taken by truck to the small town of Blerick on the west bank of the River Maas, the Dutch name for the Meuse, with which we were familiar, but in Holland it is wide, placid and slow flowing, winding through flat meadows. At Blerick it is the geographical frontier between Holland and Germany, so here we were standing on the very threshold of the Fatherland. The British 2nd Army and the Canadians had fought a long, hard campaign to get there, and we could be sure that more heavy fighting lay ahead.

For the time being, however, ours was purely a holding operation. The front line here was static. There were evidently no plans for an immediate advance, and the Germans, after their disastrous trouncing in the Ardennes, were in no condition to mount a counter-offensive. Some of their reserves had been withdrawn to face the Russians on the Eastern Front, so we just held the line, engaging in sufficient patrol activity at night to assure the Germans that we were still alert.

For the first week or two 31 Platoon was positioned on the landward perimeter of the town. We manned our slit trenches on the usual two-hours-on, four-hours-off roster, both day and night, and also stood to at dawn and dusk. For the remainder of the time we were billeted in private houses, some of which were still occupied by their owners.

Peering over the edge of my slit trench on one of the dawn stand-tos, I spotted two crouching figures creeping through the barbed wire in front of my position and in the half light recognized Major Pearman and Jem Hacker.

"Halt! Who goes there?" I yelled.

There was no response. The figures still crept forward.

"Halt, or I fire," I shouted, rattling a bullet up the spout of my Sten-gun.

Up went two pairs of hands.

"Don't shoot, Corporal," said the major, "but I thought you would have recognized us."

Jem Hacker's face was as black as thunder. He was an old enough soldier to know that I had. But there was nothing he could do about it. In fact, he told Sergeant Ashton, my platoon sergeant, that he was sure that I knew who they were but was quite right to take the action I did. The episode was widely talked over by the lads in our company and many of them asked me whether I would have fired if they had not responded to my second challenge.

"What else could I do, when two unidentified figures come creeping towards me without answering a challenge?" I asked. "Even then," I added, "They didn't give me the password."

The general opinion was that the pair would have deserved all they got.

The family in whose house I and my section were billeted consisted of a husband and wife in their mid-thirties and three young children. The family lived in the whole house except the front room downstairs, which was large and had been cleared of furniture, thus providing space for ten sleeping-bags, together with our weapons and kit. As our food came ready cooked from Company HQ, we had no need to ask for the kitchen facilities and seldom saw our hosts. Most evenings, though, we heard them when their relations or friends would come along, apparently for prayer meetings. They evidently belonged to some strict religious sect, as we could hear them chanting and praying. It got on our nerves after a time, but we reminded ourselves that we were in a friendly country and so did not interfere. It would have been interesting to learn more about them and their prayers, but we never did.

When not on duty we were free to go where we liked within our fortified perimeter. Sometimes we visited mates in other billets, for a fry-up of chips or whatever else we could scrounge, while others would come in for a game of pontoon, but we had little contact with the local inhabitants.

The exception was Tombstone, our Casanova, who, as in Civet, took a very short time to search out the local female talent. He was perpetually scrounging or bartering for presents for his latest girl. His preference was for a bar of toilet soap or, failing that, chocolate or cigarettes. He used to boast that the cheapest woman he ever bought cost him two Woodbines. As he used to leave the billet in the evenings, Jak would comment, "There goes old Tombstone — a bar of soap in one hand and a tool in the other." It was always good for a laugh.

Life was not very exciting in Blerick as, even though we were virtually in the front line, there was no imminent danger and all the bars were closed, for the Dutch had had a rough time at German hands and had no drinks to sell. Knowing the inadvisability of keeping soldiers around kicking their heels and doing nothing, the Army authorities arranged for local leave. The Americans sent their men back to Paris for weekends, while the British gave thirty-six hour passes to Brussels to those of us lucky enough to get their names drawn from a hat, and when it came to D Company's turn, who should the lucky ones be but Tombstone and myself.

A truck turned up at midday to take our fortunate party — about a dozen men from the entire battalion — on our excursion. We were to spend one night in a hostel in Brussels and be back in Blerick by midnight on the following night, when our passes expired. We had been issued with packed lunches and rode off in high spirits, singing and joking.

The hostel was a large house near the centre of the city. Tombstone and I were allocated a room with two single beds. Then the luxury of a steaming-hot bath and a change of clothing. After wallowing for as long as we dared, we dressed, brushed our hair and ate a hot meal which was by Army standards excellent. Then we were off to explore the city. Before we were allowed out, though, we were given an admonitory lecture by the sergeant in charge, who solemnly warned us against the dangers of getting drunk, having our money stolen and getting VD, which he said was rampant in Brussels. Brothels, he said, were out of bounds to us, and anyone caught there would finish up for the night in the Brussels military barracks. We listened respectfully to it all.

From bar to bar we wandered, trying to discover where the fun and the girls were. The taverns were packed, both with men from all branches of the Services and with local people. Brussels had been liberated for only five months, but already it seemed livelier and more prosperous than the wartime London we remembered. But where were the unescorted girls?

As we drifted along, getting more and more drunk and finding no feminine company at all, we began to realize that we were going to have to take a chance and go to one of those "out-of-bounds" joints. Earlier in the evening we had been accosted by several street-girls and pimps, but at that stage we were not looking for trouble. Now that we had had a change of heart, we could not find any. The girls all seemed to have left the streets. At length, a little weasel-faced man sidled up to us. "Exhibition, 60 francs," he muttered, out of the side of his mouth. It was worth a try. We followed the pimp down an alley-way and through a side door covered with a black-out curtain. In response to a knock which was obviously a code, another door opened and another pimp, who could have passed for the twin brother of the first one, asked for our 60 francs. We paid up and followed him up a flight of stairs.

The room at the top, about fifteen feet square, was dingy, to say the least. The only furniture was a double bed and a coffee table with a gramophone upon it. The window was shielded by an old army blanket tacked up in front of the curtains, and the faded wallpaper was peeling off the walls. A naked electric light bulb plumb in the centre of the ceiling provided illumination. Whatever profits were made on the "exhibitions" were certainly not spent on furniture and decorations. When we entered, there were already about a dozen men of various ranks from different units of the British 2nd Army in the room.

"Have patience, gentlemen," said the pimp in a heavily accented voice, "the exhibition is about to begin." He was too optimistic. We waited, talking and smoking, for another ten minutes or a quarter of an hour. More men came in, until there must have been twenty or thirty of us in the room. I was beginning to wonder whether the floor would stand the weight when one of the pimps closed the door and put on a gramophone record. The music was pre-war dance-band stuff.

Two women walked in. Both were in their thirties, and both wore the same gaunt, tired, hard-bitten expression. One was blonde, the other dark-haired. They started dancing around the bed and teasing the men as they stripped off their garments, one by one. The pimp kept the gramophone wound up and changed the records as necessary. When the music ceased for a moment while he was re-winding the machine, there was complete and utter silence. Then the grating chords began again.

Presently the two women stood naked before us. Both were skinny, with bony hips and sagging breasts. Not at all appetizing, but sufficiently attractive to sex-starved men who had had a few drinks and who were soon catcalling and cheering. The women then moved into the second part of their routine which was to portray the sex act in about twenty different positions. The pimp gave a running commentary on the French style, the English style, the Roman style and so on.

If I had been there alone, I think I would have been sick, but with all those men laughing and cracking coarse jokes, I laughed too. I did wonder what I was doing there, though. I am no prude, but I found the whole performance a bit disgusting. I looked at the peeling wallpaper and the blistering paint and thought how the environment matched the show. The walls were now glistening with condensation, and the temperature rose to uncomfortable levels, with all those bodies packed into such a close space. To add to the general atmosphere of sleaziness, the smell of perspiration grew steadily stronger.

After indulging in various contortions for about half an hour, the brunette disappeared, while the blonde got up, walked round the bed and snatched a black beret off a Tank Corps chap in the front rank. Taking the beret round to the men, she asked for a coin collection. The men did not know what for but most of them contributed; those who did not have coins put paper money in the hat. When she considered she had enough, she folded up the paper money very small and placed the coins very carefully on top of one another on a corner of the table. When she had a column about four inches high she lifted her leg and squatted, taking the money up inside her. Then she straightened herself and walked around for a minute or two before placing the black beret on the floor and standing over it. With knees slightly bent, she dropped the money, note by note and coin by coin, into the beret. When she had finished and the cheering had died down, she smilingly offered the men their money back. They all pulled faces and refused. So she kept it and returned the beret to the Tank Corps man. I noticed he did not put it on.

Finally she said that, as we had been a good crowd, to wind up the exhibition she would take any man who liked to offer. After a lot of hesitation and cajoling, a huge RASC corporal, six foot three and broad to match, was persuaded to have a go. Stripping off, he mounted and performed to the beat of the men's hands. Then we were all shown the door, with the exception of the corporal, whom the blonde was trying to coax to spend the night with her.

Down the stairs we all trooped, and out from the over-powering fug into the cold February night. The pimp was asking if anyone would like to visit a high-class brothel. Tombstone was keen but I was not. I asked whether it really was high class and not like the exhibition. The pimp assured us that it was, so, with some misgivings, I agreed to go.

The bar was a downstairs one, with red plush velvet banquette seating around small coffee tables. We guessed that the bedrooms were upstairs, but, as it happened, we were not to get that far. On entering we were shown to a table with four seats, and two girls came to share it with us. They were young and pretty, not at all like the other two old bags.

Tombstone, as usual where girls were concerned, took the initiative and asked what they would like to drink. It was champagne, of course. The first bottle disappeared in no time, so I ordered the next one. When it came I had a shock. It cost the equivalent of £5 a bottle — 2½ week's pay! I whispered to Tombstone that we were being taken for a ride. "We can't afford any more," I muttered. "We shall have to get them upstairs after this bottle." It was pretty futile. At the end of the second bottle the girls wanted yet another. We argued, but in the end Tombstone ordered and paid for it. That bottle too vanished just as quickly. Those girls could certainly knock it back. Whether the drinks were real champagne or not we did not know, but I did know that Tombstone was nearly broke and that, if I had to buy another bottle, so would I be. We had, of course, had quite a skinful of drinks before ever we came here, and they were beginning to make their effects felt. Tombstone was becoming maudlin and was starting to fondle his girl, whereas I was feeling argumentative.

Tombstone's girl pleaded for more champagne. I said we were sorry but we did not have any more money. Tombstone contradicted me and said he did. The girl said she only wanted one more bottle. I started arguing with Tombstone, telling him that the girls were conning us. Unfortunately Tombstone's girl, who was a right fireball, understood what I was saying. She leapt across the table and started to claw and scratch my face. To a Red Devil, accustomed to unarmed combat, a brothel girl was no opposition at all. I grabbed her wrists and threw her back across the table. Up she jumped again and started a second attack. Suddenly everyone in the bar seemed to be looking at us. Two big bouncers appeared from nowhere. This had a remarkably sobering effect on us, and especially on Tombstone, who never relished a scrap at the best of times. He waved towards the door, to signify that we were leaving quietly. We marched out in as dignified a manner as we could. The bouncers and the girls watched us go; none of them really wanted any trouble.

Out in the cold February air we looked at each other. Almost broke, there was nothing for us to do but to walk back to the hostel. The next day we spent as sober and respectable tourists, seeing the more conventional sights of Brussels. For us, the fleshpots of the city had priced themselves out of the market. Nevertheless, we had some good yarns to tell the lads back at Blerick that evening.

CHAPTER
FOURTEEN

Night Patrols

A day or two after the trip to Brussels, 31 Platoon changed places with 32 Platoon and took over an old farmhouse about a hundred yards from the river bank. All the buildings and perimeter walls of the farmyard square were of stone, and the troops who had previously occupied it had turned the place into a veritable fortress, with holes in the walls for the Bren-guns. Through our binoculars we could see the German troops in a similar fortified farmhouse half a mile or so away on their side of the river.

The buildings nearest to our farmhouse were more than a quarter of a mile away, and there was not a vestige of cover, so once inside we had to stay there till nightfall. Every evening after dark an armed party was sent back to Company HQ for a hot meal and other rations that we could warm up for ourselves during the day. In the barns were a few cows and chickens. We soon became proficient at milking the cows but decided not to kill the chickens, as most of them were laying. So, what with plenty of fresh milk and eggs, there were many worse places to spend the war than our fortified farm.

Any snow and ice there may have been on this sector of the front had vanished, but the weather was still cold and damp — the sort of cold you could feel creeping through your flesh and gripping your bones. We manned the Bren-guns on the usual two-hours-on, four-hours-off basis, plus stand-tos at dawn and dusk, but for much of the rest of the time we buried ourselves deep in the hay in the barns. My favourite post was in the hay barn, at the north-western corner of the farmstead. To get to it, we had tunnelled through about twenty yards of hay, making a passage barely wide enough for two men to pass. If the barn had been set on fire in an attack, the position would have been a death trap.

However, all remained quiet, apart from an occasional shell, lobbing across the river. There were German patrols about, but they never came near us. Our only immediate hazard revealed itself when I was sitting in my warm nest one night and felt something land on my head. It was so heavy that my head swayed to and fro under the weight. I realized that it must be a rat, and a big one at that. I flicked my head, and the rat fell off. I heard it scrambling away through the hay. Later we found that the place was infested with rats, but we took little notice of them. Live and let live was our attitude towards them, as long as they did not help themselves to our rations. We had enough killing on our hands without bothering about them.

Once during this period there was the arrival, overnight, of dozens of propaganda leaflets. No one heard anything — neither plane nor shell nor patrol —

137

but there they were in the morning, scattered all over the farmyard. The front depicted a pretty blonde in the nude; the back showed her in bed with a man, whose civilian clothes hung from a peg on the bedroom door. The caption read: "Why stay fighting in a foreign land when your best friend is sleeping with your wife or girl friend while you are protecting them? Why don't you desert and find out exactly what is going on back home?" The attempt at propaganda was so ingenuous and amateurish that it was almost an insult to our intelligence. Still, it was good for a laugh. The nude blonde made a good pin-up, and we plastered her picture all over the farmyard.

Meanwhile other units farther up the river had been sending patrols across the river at night, trying to pick up a prisoner to learn what enemy units, and in what strength, were facing us. So far they had had no success, so it was decided to try from the base afforded by our farmhouse.

First of all, eight volunteers from our platoon were needed to act as a boat party. They were to be on duty for about four hours each night and so were excused other night duties. There was no shortage of volunteers, as the jaunt offered a chance of excitement and was better than the dull routine of the farmyard. I was chosen to be one of them, and so was Sergeant Ashton, who was to lead the party.

The first night we carried the canvas boat down to the river and quietly launched it. Four men, under Sergeant Ashton, paddled the boat across, with an officer and a lance-corporal of A Company on board.

The other four, under my charge, remained on the west bank to give covering fire if necessary. The boat party had two Bren-guns and two rifles, and so did we. The officer and the lance-corporal disembarked on the far bank and disappeared. The boat returned to us.

Every hour, on the hour, for the next three hours the boat party silently paddled the boat across, but the patrol was never on the opposite bank to meet them and eventually had to be given up as lost. Meantime my party took it in turns to dig a series of slit trenches. We worked as quietly as possible and threw the surplus earth into the river. As the trenches were on top of the bank, I was pretty sure the Germans would not spot them, even in daylight.

Next night we repeated the exercise across the river, with another officer and corporal, but this time it was my turn to lead the boat party. Charlie Ashton had briefed me on what to look for. We had to paddle obliquely upstream until halfway across, then let the current take us, still paddling, in the direction of a church tower that was silhouetted against the skyline. The current in midstream was much stronger than we had anticipated and carried us below our target, but, once out of the main stream, we were able to paddle back to the correct spot on the German bank. Providentially the night was very dark, with no moon. I whispered good luck to the lieutenant, with whom I had previously synchronized watches. Three times, on the hour, we paddled back across the river to the rendezvous and waited for exactly two minutes, but no one came.

This went on for six consecutive nights, and not once did a patrol return. All had to be presumed lost.

On the seventh night it was D Company's turn to produce volunteers for the patrol. The mission was obviously so hazardous that the volunteers were promised that, if they returned with a prisoner, the officer would receive the Military Cross (which can be awarded only to officers) and the corporal the Military Medal. Bill Collins asked me if I would have a go with him, and I agreed. But Lieutenant Weeks and Corporal Tom Jones had got in first, so they were given preference to have first try.

Weeks, who was one of the bravest of junior officers, came over in daylight on a motorcycle to our farmhouse, something we were not allowed to do, but he wanted to get what first-hand information he could from our boat parties and look at the terrain in daylight. He also spent a long time studying the far side of the river with his binoculars. This made a lot of sense to me, and I was rather surprised that none of the other officers had taken the same precaution before going on patrol. I made a mental note that, if and when it was my turn, I would do the same. We already had a map of the German territory. I saw that Weeks was sketching on it the shapes of the houses and anything else that was likely to show up as shapes in the night. He proposed to memorize it before setting out that evening.

Weeks suggested a change of plan. He said that he would prefer the boat party to stay on the British side, to give covering fire if needed, while he and Jones

140

paddled the boat across themselves. He had decided just where he would land the boat, and he would leave it tied up there so they could pick it up and paddle themselves back at the end of their mission. He was convinced that he needed to keep the means of escape on his side of the river. We nodded. It was his decision, and it was his life. Weeks, moreover, was well thought of by his own men, who were sure that, if anyone could bring off this hazardous quest, he would.

So, at half-past ten that night, our boat party, with Weeks and Jones, all with blackened faces, left the farmyard, carrying the collapsible canvas boat. We crept noiselessly down to the river bank, and Weeks and Jones climbed in. Facing the boat upstream, we gave it a push, and in no time at all it was out of sight in the darkness. Before a minute was up, we could no longer hear even the tiny muffled splashes of the paddles. So we retired to our slit trenches and waited.

Time passed slowly. Ten minutes, twenty minutes, half an hour, forty minutes. Then, just on the stroke of three-quarters of an hour, we heard a distant burst of machine-gun fire. It was followed by silence, but two or three minutes later there was shouting on the far bank and more machine-gun fire. This last was certainly German; there was no mistaking the rapid fire of an MG 42. Suddenly a flare illuminated the sky. In a light almost as bright as day I could see the boat in the middle of the stream, with one man paddling for all he was worth. German machine-guns opened up, and spurts of water erupted all around the boat. But the flare and the tracer bullets had revealed to us where the

German gunners were, and we let them have it with our Bren-guns. Charlie Ashton shouted, "Forget your rifles. Just keep those Bren-guns going with rapid fire. We've plenty of full magazines with us." The row was deafening, but our fire was effective. The German gunners became less accurate and more spasmodic, and no more water volcanoes erupted anywhere near the boat.

As the flare died down, the paddler in the boat was seen to be growing very tired and to be losing his battle with the current. So Ashton shouted to the four Bren-gunners to remain with their guns and for the rest of us to bring our rifles and follow him downstream. After about a hundred yards we were able to wade into the river, reach the boat, drag it to the shore and then tow it back to the original landing-point. It had shipped several inches of water, which was pouring in through the bullet holes made by the machine-gun fire, but Lieutenant Weeks scrambled out unhurt.

Corporal Jones, however, was wounded. Bill Collins had had the forethought to send down some first-aid men with stretchers as soon as he had heard the firing. They lifted Jones out and laid him on a stretcher. He looked in a bad way, with a bullet wound in the neck, but he sounded quite cheerful. "Best of luck for tomorrow night, Andy," he said to me.

The stretcher-bearers carried him by hand all the way back to the casualty clearing centre, a trek of several miles. With a bullet in his neck, they were afraid to trust him to motor transport. A jolt might have killed him. Unfortunately, I never heard whether he survived or not.

Back at the farm Lieutenant Weeks told us what had happened. During his long study of the terrain on the previous day he had noticed a detached house which the enemy seemed to be using. So he and Jones had made straight for this house and gone inside. The ground floor seemed to be deserted, but they could hear movement upstairs. Suddenly a German came clattering down the stairs and threw open the door of the room in which they were crouching. Weeks stuck a Sten-gun into his stomach and whispered for him to keep quiet. Unfortunately for the German, the shock must have been too great, as he inadvertently gave a yell. Weeks had no alternative but to squeeze the trigger, and then he and Jones had to run for it. They had already reached the boat and started to paddle across when the Germans opened fire. Jones was hit by the first burst, and Weeks had to do all the paddling. He did not give much for his chances when the flare went up, and he was sure he would have been a dead duck if it had not been for our covering fire. He shrugged, thanked us for our support, wished Bill Collins the best of luck for the next night and went back to Company HQ to report.

Naturally, as we sat around on the hay, eating our canned sausages and beans for breakfast, the night's episode was the chief topic of conversation. Everyone was speculating as to how Bill Collins and myself would get on during the coming night. As for me, I was beginning to get cold feet and was wondering how I had allowed myself to be talked into volunteering.

However, any anxiety was, I felt, pointless, as before lunch we received a message telling us to be ready to move at dusk. We were going back to England.

At first there was considerable elation, but that was before we knew why we were going home. We were to be the spearhead of a new attack — an airborne assault to proceed the crossing of the Rhine. We were to force the last great barrier between the Allies and the heart of the Fatherland.

Even from our post by the Mass we could see, every now and again in the north-western sky, the trail of V2 rockets ascending like brilliant stars into the night sky. They were being fired from the bases which the Germans still held in northern Holland and were heading for London, where my parents were living.

"The sooner we can get this lot over, the better," I thought, "before Hitler comes up with any more of his secret weapons."

CHAPTER
FIFTEEN

Respite and Refit

So, rather more than two months after we had left England to join in the Battle of the Bulge, we were on our way home again. We handed over our positions at Blerick to American infantry and went by truck to Brussels Airport, and then flew in a Dakota to Lyneham, in Wiltshire, where we found lorries waiting to take us the final twenty miles or so to our old camp on Salisbury Plain.

Here we started to refit in preparation for the next operation. There were kit inspections, and men with shortages had to go to the stores and make good the deficiencies in clothing and equipment at their own expense. All marching-boots had to be sent to the battalion cobblers for re-studding, and rifles were tested for accuracy. A hundred and one things were checked, to make sure that we were fully ready again for instant action.

Everything was in a hustle and bustle, and a feeling of excitement and apprehension pervaded the camp. We had had no official briefing about the next operation, but everyone assumed that it would be the Rhine crossing, which none of the officers denied. It must have been one of the worst-kept secrets of the war, and it became even more obvious when, after a few days, the battalion took part in an exercise on the flat plains of Lincolnshire. It had to be more than a coincidence that the countryside here was much the same as in the northern Rhineland.

It was a pity that this final exercise in our programme was spoiled for me by an unpleasant incident. Returning to camp on the evening of the third day, I found myself on duty as company orderly corporal and was asked by the quartermaster to send two men from every platoon to the cookhouse to wash up all the cooking-equipment that had been used. It was a rotten chore to order men to do at ten o'clock in the evening, as most were in bed or having a drink at the NAAFI. However, I was able to find two men available in each of the platoons until I arrived at my own hut.

Opening the door, I could see that there were only two men in the hut who had not yet gone to bed. One was "Offie" Moore, quite a close friend of mine who was called "Offie" because he was always devising schemes for escaping parades. The other was Harold Newing, who had dressed my wounds in the Battle of Normandy and helped carry me back to the first-aid post. I told them what was required, adding that I was sorry but the job had to be done and the sooner they got it finished the sooner they could go to bed. Offie Moore, despite his reputation, agreed, but to my surprise Harold Newing refused point-blank. Offie tried to persuade him, but to no avail. I then repeated the order, and Newing again refused.

"Now look here," I said. "I've ordered you twice to get down to that cookhouse, and you've refused. I'm now going to order you for the third time, and you know that, if you refuse, I'll have to put you in the guard room."

"You've no right to order me to the cookhouse at this time of night, and I'm still refusing," was the reply.

By this time several of the men who had either been asleep or were pretending to be asleep were sitting up and taking notice. Some of them tried to persuade Newing to do the job, and one even volunteered to do it instead of him, but I knew I could not afford to give way as, if I did, my authority would never be worth a farthing.

"You," I said, pointing to the chap who had volunteered, "can go down to the cookhouse and help Offie."

The man got dressed without argument and followed Offie, who, sensing trouble, had already vanished.

"Now you and you," I pointed to two others, "get dressed, take your rifles and escort Private Newing to the guard room with me."

Again there was no argument. No one said a word, and within a few minutes I had them formed up, one escort in front, one at the rear, and Harold Newing in the middle.

"Quick march to the guard room, left, right, left, right." And off we went to the guard room, where Newing was locked up for the night.

I dismissed the two men and returned to company office, where I had to stay on duty all night. I felt badly about it all and kept turning the matter over in my mind. But what else could I have done, I asked myself, and always came back to the same answer. There had been no alternative. It was going to be a long night, I thought, alone with my misgivings. I had just decided to make myself a cup of tea when the door burst open and in strode Arthur Newing.

"You're a right bastard, you are!" he shouted. "My brother and I rescued you when you were wounded, and this is how you pay him back. You blokes are all the same once you get a couple of stripes on your arm."

"Unless I get an apology from you, Newing, you'll join your brother in the guard room," I snapped, quietly. It was probably the quietness of my tone that stopped him short. He had obviously expected a slanging match. "I don't even have to caution you. I could put you under arrest now if I wanted to," I continued in a normal voice. "But I don't want to, any more than I wanted to put your brother in the guard room." I explained what had happened. "I'm as sorry as you are about the way it turned out, particularly after what you did for me in Normandy, but he disobeyed an order in front of other men and left me with no alternative. If the same thing occurred tomorrow, I would have to do just the same. Both you and your brother have been around long enough to know that."

Arthur Newing grunted. "All right," he said, "let's forget it. But don't expect me to apologize."

"You either apologize, or you're in the guard room yourself," I replied. I hated myself for turning the knife in the wound, but I knew that I could not let Newing get away with it or he would have gone back to the hut boasting that he had straightened things out with that bastard of an orderly corporal. "Come on, let's have your apology," I continued briskly, "and then we'll forget about it."

"I'm sorry, Corporal," muttered Newing ungraciously under his breath as he rushed out of the hut slamming the door. My first inclination was to call him back, but I decided to let him go. Enough was enough.

Just before eight o'clock next morning Harold Newing, two escorts and myself reported to the regimental sergeant-major at Battalion HQ. The offence had been considered serious enough to be tried by Colonel Charlton, the battalion commander, rather than by Major Pearman.

The RSM lined us up, first me, then Newing with an escort on either side.

"Escort and accused, quick march, left-right, left-right," barked the RSM, and as we marched before the CO he snatched Newing's red beret from his head. "Halt. Right turn."

We all turned and, except Newing, saluted and stood at attention.

"Corporal, I understand you are bringing a charge against Private Newing," said Colonel Charlton in a brisk but kindly manner. "Please state your case."

I stated my case. The colonel looked at Newing.

"What have you to say about this charge?" he asked.

Newing had obviously been considering matters during his hours in the guard room.

"Nothing, sir, only that I'm very sorry it happened. It won't happen again, sir."

"Well, make sure it doesn't. I find you guilty, and that will mean seven days confined to the guard room and fourteen days' loss of pay. That's all."

"Right turn," barked the RSM. "Quick march, left-right, left-right." As we went out of the door, he handed Newing back his red beret with the comment, "And don't let me see you here again."

Newing and his escort marched back to the guard room, and the RSM turned to me.

"Well done, Corporal," he said. "I wish more of our young NCOs were as firm as you. I'll have my eye on you for future promotion. Dismiss."

But that, of course, was not what I was after, and I was still feeling unhappy as I walked back to D Company lines. Being congratulated by Jem Hacker did not help to cheer me up.

The reason why the colonel had given Newing such a short sentence, though making it more severe by stopping his pay, soon became apparent. Just about a week later the whole battalion was sent on leave for ten days, and he did not want him to forfeit his leave just before being sent into action.

I spent my leave at home, though as none of my old friends were about, I found little to do; however, I enjoyed being looked after by my family. The flying bombs had ceased, and people were beginning to anticipate the end of the war, but after a week I started to look forward to getting back to the Red Devils. I was not at all eager for more action and felt considerably cheered by a headline in the papers on 8th March which reported that the American 1st Army had captured a bridge over the Rhine at Remagen. Perhaps, after all, we would not now be needed to carry out an airborne crossing of the river.

Forty-eight hours after our return to camp we knew better.

The first move was to a camp on an airfield in north Essex, and we were largely confined for briefing. And what a briefing that was! It was far more detailed and accurate than anything we had ever previously encountered. It was backed up with maps, large-scale aerial photographs and details of all the enemy units expected to be in the vicinity of our targets. The planners had really gone to town.

They had every incentive. We were told that, after the failure at Arnhem, the politicians and, even more important, the public — would not stand for another tragedy, such as would occur if the land forces again failed to link up with the airborne troops across the Rhine. The plan therefore was that the 6th Airborne Division would take off from England and the American 17th Airborne Division from airfields in France and land eight or ten miles east of the Rhine, providing that the commandos and other land forces had secured a bridgehead on the east bank. If the bridgehead had not been achieved, then the air armadas would turn back, even though they were airborne.

The 24th March was the date for the land assault. The commandos would cross the Rhine in the early hours, being ferried across in landing-craft manned by the Royal Navy. In this sector the river was more than a quarter of a mile wide with a five-knot current, so it was quite a formidable barrier to cross. As the land on either side was flat with no cover and criss-crossed by streams and canals, the assault was obviously not going to be easy. According to our briefing, as soon as the ground troops had gained a foothold, our glider troops which would be the first wave in were to clear dropping zones for two parachute brigades.

Our battalion was to capture the small town of Haminkeln, some ten miles east of the Rhine. It stood at important crossroads, controlling roads which led to the proposed main battle area. We had to take these road junctions and deny their use to the enemy, who would be needing them to bring up reserves of men and ammunition. East of the town was a smaller river, spanned by two bridges which were our secondary objectives as they would be required, once the bridge-head over the Rhine had been consolidate, by our armoured columns to advance across the North German Plain.

The briefing was so thorough that it took nearly three days. Every man in the battalion was told in detail the role and duty of every company and also the tasks of each platoon in his own company. 31 Platoon was set the task of taking the southern road junction, and it was left to the platoon commander to break down our duties into even further detail, so that every man knew exactly what was expected of him.

My section was given one corner of the crossroads to capture. It included one large house and several smaller ones. From large-scale maps and aerial photographs we were shown just where the doors and windows were, the front door of the big house being right on the corner of the road junction. We were, on landing, to run to the house, stand with our backs to the wall and give covering fire to other sections. Then I had to throw a grenade through the right-hand window, and Harry Harris had to throw one through the left-hand window. After both had exploded, I was to shoot through the lock with my Sten-gun, and the whole section would burst into the house. Harry Harris, Joe Mullins, Jakoff, Jack Nichols and Ted Lockey were to search and clear the whole of the ground floor, while Ponsonby, Tombstone, Alfie Ross (the Bren-gunner) and Ray Best (his no. 2) were to storm the upper floor with me. Once the house was cleared, the Bren-gun would be installed at the window over the front door, while the others and I would clear the adjoining houses and link up with other sections. Thus eventually the entire village would be cleared.

We were enormously impressed. An operation planned in such detail, involving so much intelligence information, could hardly fail. Our morale rode high.

The briefing was followed by stern warnings. As we were now going to fight in enemy territory, there was to be no fraternizing with the civilian population, and especially with those of the opposite sex. We could expect to find mines and booby traps in any building we entered and must be on our guard day and night.

We were further told that the enemy troops defending the sector were the élite German 1st Parachute Army, who could be expected to defend their Fatherland with fanatical zeal. We wcre to take no chances with them, and no one was to wander off on his own. No quarter could be expected, and none was to be given.

As we were to be landed ahead of the ground troops, even though the distance between us was short, it might be two or three days before we could make contact. We were to travel light, each of us with only a twenty-four-ration pack. Once that was gone, we would have to live off whatever we could find. We were also warned that there was always a risk that food or water might be contaminated, so we were told to exercise the greatest care. We were issued with water-purification kits, which consisted of two bottles of tablets, one to purify the water and the other to take away the foul taste that resulted. Even then, all water was to be boiled. Finally, in case the link-up took longer than expected, we were given Benzedrine pills to keep us awake. In the event of our having to keep alert for three or four consecutive days and nights, we were to take the pills whenever we felt tired.

Some extra items of kit were of unusual interest. They included escape equipment, consisting of small waterproof maps of western Europe, which we were to sew into the linings of our battledress; also hacksaw blades six inches long and a quarter of an inch wide. I sewed mine into the seam over my fly buttons. We also had two brass buttons, which superficially resembled the ordinary ones on Army trousers. One of them, when inverted, had a small spike projecting from the centre, while the other, again when inverted, had a recess in the centre which fitted over the spike. On the reverse of this second one was a blob of phosphorous. When the buttons were placed one on the other, they made a small but reasonably accurate compass.

We were reminded that, if we were captured, our first duty was to escape. On previous campaigns we had been operating in countries occupied by the Germans, where the chances of the population helping us were high. In the coming operation, however, the chances of help from civilians were virtually nil. So, if we were taken prisoner and managed to escape, we were advised to travel by night and hide by day.

In the intervals between this extraordinarily thorough briefing we found time for some football, and in the evenings we were able to organize concerts. The relaxation cheered us up and helped to pass the time, but beneath it we were on edge. Again my mind was filled with doubts and apprehension. No matter how many times I went into action, I felt as nervous as on the first occasion. Would I come out alive this time? Would I be all in one piece? Experience had by now taught me that I would not let myself or my men down by showing cowardice, but I dreaded the possibility of again being wounded. Also, with the war nearing its end, I preferred not to get killed. Life is always the sweeter the nearer you are to losing it.

I guessed that the thoughts of my comrades were working along the same lines, but as usual we never discussed them. I am sure, though, that we were all regretting that the opposition was to be that crack German 1st Parachute Army. What a battle this was going to be! The greatest river assault in history. The British 21st Army Group were, we were told, to deploy something like a million and a quarter men. And how many men, I wondered, are required to support one man at the front? I had heard various figures, from one-in-ten, to one-in-a-hundred, and it seemed to me that the average soldier's chances of having to carry a rifle and take part in a bayonet charge were fairly remote.

Things began to move fast. The time for reflection was at an end. After an early breakfast on 24th March we assembled our battle equipment and packed the rest of our gear into our kitbags, for transit back to Salisbury Plain. I never saw my kitbag again.

CHAPTER SIXTEEN

Over the Rhine

At seven-thirty that morning we were on parade for roll-call, and by eight o'clock we were formed up alongside the gliders, ready to embark for take-off at eight-thirty.

I was not too happy when my section was ordered to be first aboard our glider. It meant that we should be sitting in the middle, while the two exits were at either end. It is bad enough sitting in an airborne glider with enemy aircraft and anti-aircraft guns taking a pot at you, but it is even worse once the glider has landed. A glider on the ground is the ultimate sitting duck, and the Germans, unlike British sporting gentry, had no compunction about shooting at a sitting bird.

The gliders incorporated an innovation. Once the two pilots had vacated the cockpit, the nose of the glider could be blown off by a small explosive charge. This enabled ramps to be placed in position at the front, so that the handcart could quickly be got out and the men at the front could get out in about half the previous time.

So there we were at last, the entire 31 Platoon, sitting in our glider, with our backs to the fuselage. We were all

157

strapped in tight, but we had no parachutes as on our earlier flights. The handcart, which held the PIAT mortar, its bombs and other equipment too heavy for men to carry, was strapped to the centre of the floor. Outside, the towing planes were revving up, and for the first time we noticed that four-engined Halifax bombers had replaced the old twin-engined Whitleys. We were also promised complete air support and immunity from the Luftwaffe all the vay to the target, such was the air supremacy that the Allies had now achieved.

As we climbed over the Essex countryside, those of us near the portholes looked out and watched a prodigious armada of tow planes and gliders with their escorts, as far as the eye could see. The air fleet, over five thousand strong, was, in fact, carrying well over twenty thousand men to destinations behind the enemy lines, probably the largest airborne expedition of all time.

The 3½-hour flight to the Rhine seemed to us the longest 3½ hours we had ever known. The glider had no radio, so we had no idea whether everything was going to plan. We would only know that the operation was called off (as we still hoped!) if the planes turned round and started for home. But no such luck. Still, as Bill Collins said, if the airborne operation was halted, it could only be because the Allied ground attack had been stopped, and that would mean a lot of dead and wounded down below. We would not want that to happen.

When we had passed beyond the Essex coast and its mud-flats and were well out over the North Sea, everyone seemed so glum and preoccupied that Sergeant Charlie Ashton called on Ken Edwards to go through his repertoire of jokes. Ken, who was doubtless feeling anything but light-hearted, found the going hard at first, but gradually he warmed up, reeling off all the good old ribald Army jokes, and what with them and the songs, in which we all joined, our spirits rose a little.

Over the Dutch coast Bill Collins asked all section leaders to inspect their men's weapons. This had already been done about three times that morning, but there was no harm in going through the motions again. The Bren-guns were dismantled and reassembled; the magazines were checked to ensure they were full; the riflemen all pulled through their rifles and checked that their magazines held the maximum ten rounds; the section leaders went through their Sten-guns, their bandoliers, grenades, the PIAT mortar and the two-inch mortar. After that, we checked our personal equipment — knives, field dressings, twenty-four-hour ration packs, water-purification sets, toggle ropes, escape aids, webbing and everything we could think of. It helped to pass the time and, more important, kept our minds off the immediate future. Not long after the checks were completed, we saw smoke rising in the distance ahead. Then, far away and far below, the silver streak of the River Rhine came into view. Certainly there could be no turning back now.

As we approached the Rhine, we realized that the smoke was rising from the battle raging down there. And with it came the realization that those meticulous planners had made an awful omission. What they had failed to take into account was that our vast fleet of slow, cumbersome gliders would pass only a thousand feet or so above a battlefield.

It was all very well to assure us that we would not have to land until the ground troops had obtained a foothold on the east bank of the Rhine. But the route we were taking ensured that the whole German Army, engaged in battle down below, had a splendid view of us. Immediately we had crossed the Rhine we came under fire from German anti-aircraft guns and machine-guns. Peering out of the portholes, I could see puffs of smoke as flak exploded between the planes and gliders. The German gunners had a field day. We were travelling at only about a hundred miles an hour, and, because of our numbers we had no room for manœuvre or even to take evasive action. Not that there is much that tow planes and gliders can do without risking the tow ropes breaking.

However, we did manœuvre quite a lot, involuntarily, as the blast of the flak shells threw the gliders about the sky, like small boats in a turbulent sea. It was fortunate that the gliders, being made of plywood, could take an enormous amount of that sort of punishment. From my peep-hole I saw two of them hit. One had a wing almost shot off; the other had its tail plane and rudder badly damaged. The only thing the glider pilots could do was to cast off from the tow planes and try to make the best possible landing. Then I saw three tow planes hit, all of them going down in flames. Their glider pilots had to cast off as quickly as they could, to save themselves from being dragged earthwards. They would then have to try to get as near as they could to the specified landing-zone or at least endeavour to avoid coming down in the middle of the German Army. While watching these absorbing events I could see tracer bullets racing up from the ground towards us. I swear that some of them came within three feet of my porthole.

We were not surprised to learn later that the losses suffered by the glider-borne troops were enormous. To send us at such a low altitude directly over the battle zone was either a shocking error of judgement or a calculated risk. Until now we had been in no hurry to land in Germany; now we could not hit the deck fast enough. Looking back, I remember that, as when at other times in action I had been in mortal danger, I did not feel afraid. It all seemed so unreal. It was not I who was sitting there, watching the flak shells and tracer bullets all around. It was someone else in my body, and I was looking at him from the outside. I was simply a spectator. It was a weird sensation. Perhaps that is what happens when one dies.

Now we encountered another hazard, as the Germans put down a dense smoke screen for miles around the dropping-zone. It was aided by a certain amount of ground fog and, as our glider started its descent, one of the pilots called back to Bill Collins that he could not guarantee to put us down in the right place. The best he could do was to find a gap in the smoke and fog and try to land the glider in any field that happened to be visible. So much for our meticulous briefing!

The smoke screen deceived our pilots about their altitude, and the ground came rushing up to meet us much faster than they expected or intended. By their united efforts of hauling on the joysticks with all their strength, they were able to check our dive to perdition. We levelled out to make a fast, bumpy but safe landing. Machine-gun and rifle fire was cracking and crackling all around, and our glider received several hits the moment it landed. We all spilled out the front and back, leaving the handcart behind, on Bill Collins' orders. We could come back for that later, if all went well. Meantime we had to disperse as quickly as possible.

We had landed in the corner of a large field. Those of us who dropped out of the rear of the glider ran like mad to a ditch alongside an elevated road about a hundred yards away. Those who emerged from the front had seen a closer hedge and ditch about fifty yards from the glider's nose. I was with the first lot. There we were, lying in the ditch, with the road bank towering above us, while Lieutenant Bill Collins tried to work out where we were from his map. With no landmarks visible, it was an impossible task. Yet somehow we had to find our way to Haminkeln as quickly as possible.

Telling us to stay where we were, Bill Collins crawled to the top of the embankment with his map and binoculars. Then he committed a brave but suicidal act by standing up to get a better view. He was immediately hit and fell face downwards, with his body lying at an unnatural angle on the top of the bank. I did not have to risk my life to see whether his pulse was still beating. He was lying in one of those grotesque positions only assumed by the dead.

So there we were, newly landed in enemy territory, with no officer, no binoculars, no map and still under sniper fire.

There were about twenty of us, and I was the only NCO. I thought that the best thing we could do would be to try to link up with Charlie Ashton in the ditch across the field. So, telling the others to follow, I crept along the ditch to the place where ditch and hedge met. There I found half a dozen men, stragglers from other gliders, but no sergeant. However, a moment later two men came rolling down the bank. They were Colonel Charlton and his batman.

"Who's in charge here?" demanded the colonel, struggling to his feet. Nobody answered. "Speak up, someone," barked the colonel.

"I don't know whether I'm the senior NCO, sir," I said, "but our platoon commander has been killed, and the platoon sergeant has been cut off, and we've no maps."

"Who are you, then?" asked the colonel.

"Corporal Anderson, 31 Platoon, D Company, sir."

The colonel looked at my arm and saw the marks where I had stripped off my stripes in the glider, to hide my rank. This was standard practice, though not strictly permissible, as the enemy always tried to pick off the officers and NCOs first. I glanced at the shoulders of the colonel's shirt and saw he had got rid of his insignia too.

"Ah, I remember," said the colonel. "You brought that man in on a charge a few weeks ago."

"Yes, sir."

"Right, then," the colonel was spreading out his map. "This is where we are now. I believe your objective is the southern end of the town, about a mile up the road," and he pointed to the location on his map. I nodded agreement. "We can't wait for any more men," continued the colonel. "We'll probably be joined by a few stragglers on the way, and we'll just have to manage with what we've got."

He told us that he had set up battalion HQ in a farmyard but, being unable to make contact with anyone by radio, had come to try to find out at first hand what was happening. He was wearing his red beret rather than his steel helmet (and that too was against regulations). He had discarded his flying-smock and battledress and was dressed only in his slacks and shirt, with the sleeves rolled up. The unfortunate batman was carrying the rest of the colonel's gear in addition to his own — but then he was only about half the colonel's age.

By the time we were ready to move, more men had joined us, and we now mustered nearly fifty, to capture the town of Haminkeln with its vital road junctions — an undertaking for which our planners had allocated five hundred men. But I got the impression that our determined colonel was quite prepared to attempt it, single-handed if necessary.

The Germans had snipers covering almost every section of the elevated roadway. However, there were houses that might offer cover at intervals of about two hundred yards or so along the road. So the colonel told us to leap-frog from one to another, spacing ourselves from five to ten yards apart, running like hares and only regrouping when we arrived at the outskirts of the town.

"I'll go first," he said; "then my batman; then you," pointing at me. "The rest of you follow, and for God's sake don't stop running till you're under cover. We'll break into every house on the way and hope to God the Jerries have only got small arms and that there aren't any tanks or artillery to shell the houses. Best of luck. See you in Haminkeln." With that he was off, followed a second or so later by his batman.

Before I followed him, I yelled to my section. "All get up from the bank in different places when your turn comes. If you all take the same route, Jerry will draw a bead on that position, and you'll have had it." The ones I could see nodded. "OK. Let's go," I yelled, and I scrambled up the bank.

The colonel and the batman were now twenty or thirty yards ahead, and I made after them as fast as my legs could carry me. This is where my running prowess, improved by all those cross-country runs, served me well. I had gained a lot on the batman by the time we reached the first house; indeed, I was only about five yards behind him. I dived through a gap in a hedge, wriggled on my stomach to the door and moved quickly inside.

The house had been evacuated, and I wondered where the owners had gone. Even now, in the heat of battle, I found time to puzzle over the inexplicable disappearance of civilians when a battle reached their homes. I had noticed it in the Ardennes and in Normandy. Even more surprising was the way in which they reappeared and started to pick up the threads of their lives as soon as the shooting had passed.

The colonel was already knocking out the window frame on the opposite side of the house. Through the window he climbed and was off on the next lap of his mad journey. The batman and I followed. Behind me I could hear footsteps and hoped that the rest of the platoon were still coming on, but there was no time even to turn my head to see as it was a good two hundred yards, probably more, to the next house, which occupied a bend in the road. Wherever the German snipers were, they had evidently realized that the long gap between the two houses was going to be their best opportunity and concentrated their fire about ten yards from the house which was our objective.

The colonel made it safely, but his batman went down about ten yards from safety.

"Don't stop!" the colonel yelled to me.

I had no intention of doing so. Two cracks, as one bullet whizzed past my ankles and another uncomfortably near my head, provided an incentive to continue moving at top speed. Then Joe Mullins, the big cockney lad in my section, who was immediately behind me, went down.

"Pass the message on to leave the killed and wounded," shouted the colonel. "They'll get looked after as soon as possible. We must move on. Every second is vital."

From the house on the bend we could see the buildings on the fringe of the town and that with two or three more frantic dashes we would reach their cover. The road was now lined by trees, and these and the bend made things rather difficult for the snipers, but we lost three more men before we gained the safety of the first house in town, where we found the colonel waiting for us.

He outlined our next moves. He would lead half the men up the right-hand side of the road, and he ordered me to lead the rest up the other side. Remembering our training in street fighting, we knew exactly what to do. The colonel advanced to the first doorway, while my men and I, with our backs to the wall on the other side of the road, covered every doorway and window on his side. When he was safely in position, it was our turn to advance, while he covered us. So, doorway by doorway, house by house, we crept forward.

Suddenly machine-gun fire spurted from an upstairs window just ahead. I burst open the front door of the next house on our side, closely followed by Ponsonby and Tombstone. They ran upstairs and began firing at the house from which the firing had come, while I, at a ground-floor window, pointed it out to the colonel. Keeping close to the wall, he took three men forward,

167

inching along with their backs to the wall. When they arrived at the manned house, on which we were keeping up a constant fire, they tossed grenades through the front door. Just to make sure, one of the men dashed to the middle of the road, lobbed a grenade into the upstairs window and leaped back to cover again. As soon as the grenades had exploded, the three men ran into the house. I heard a rattle of gunfire from inside, then the men emerged, covered with dust but unhurt. Meantime I resumed the advance on my side of the road. Several more times as we made our way along the street, we encountered similar hold-ups, but each was dealt with in the same manner.

Presently I recognized, from the large-scale aerial photographs I had seen, the first crossroads that was our original objective and then, suddenly, we were in the main square of Haminkeln. The square was dominated by a large building over which a swastika was flying, but as it had not been one of the original objectives of 31 Platoon, I had no information about its purpose, though it looked as if it could be a strong-point.

"Corporal," shouted the colonel from across the road, "that's the anti-aircraft headquarters. Take your section and clear it while I carry on through the town."

Taking the first seven men of my section, I dashed across to the building and tossed grenades in at the ground and first floors. We did not risk throwing any at the upper floors in case we missed and they rebounded on us. We flattened ourselves against the outside walls of the buildings until the grenades exploded; then in we went. We found that the house had a central staircase. Telling Harry Harris and Ray Best to clear the ground floor, I started up the stairs, followed by the others. At the first floor I left behind Jack Nichols and Ted Lockey, to clear that level; at the second, Tombstone and Jakoff. That left Ponsonby and myself to deal with the attic. Frank followed me up the narrow stairway, ready for anything, but the birds had flown. Only their commander remained, and as I burst into the attic, I was confronted by a German SS captain, who saluted and handed me his Walther automatic pistol, butt first.

The room was about twelve feet square, with windows on all sides. The tables were littered with maps, and a radio transmitter was crackling with static until I silenced it with a burst of Sten-gun fire. I handed the officer over to Ponsonby, with instructions to search him carefully and then take him and the maps to the colonel as fast as possible. I then went quickly through the contents of the attic and found a Schmeisser sub-machine carbine and dagger, with the SS insignia and swastika on it, and this I tucked inside my belt. Finally I pulled down the German flag from the roof and stowed it inside my flying-smock. It would make a splendid souvenir.

We had taken about ten minutes to clear the building, or rather to search it to make sure there were no lurking enemy. The Germans had evidently moved out while there was still time, — all except the commander, who had probably been operating his transmitter until the last minute. I called on the other men to follow me, and so we went out into the town square. No one fired at us, and, indeed, there was no sound of gunfire in the town at all — only the distant noise of battle far away to the west.

So there we were, in control of our objective. We had done what we had been briefed to do, but with about one-tenth of the number of men the planners had calculated we would need. It was yet another case of well-trained men under inspired leadership achieving the seemingly impossible.

CHAPTER
SEVENTEEN

Cold Steel

Needless to say, the colonel did not wait for us to complete our task in the anti-aircraft headquarters. By the time we came out into the square again, he had reached the edge of the town and linked up with C Company, which, like us, had landed off target and had had to fight their way into Haminkeln. It was now 3p.m., just three hours after the first gliders had landed. The whole town was in our hands, and now we had to hold it till the ground forces arrived. We set about preparing defensive positions. Old cars, trucks, carts — anything movable was dragged into position to form road-blocks guarding the approaches to the two vital crossroads.

Throughout the afternoon we had a steady stream of reinforcements, as glider troops who had lost their way came straggling in. Among them were Sergeant Ashton and the remnants of D Company, who had had to fight a battle with a German patrol and had suffered casualties. Also among the newcomers were a few glider pilots, mainly RAF pilots, who, because of a surplus, had taken an extra course in piloting gliders. They told me that they had all received weapon training too and were at our disposal until the ground troops arrived. Then they were under orders to make their way back to headquarters, ready for further airborne operations. I admired their spirit.

No news came of the other companies, nor did we have any information about the progress of the land forces. It did seem, though, that the two glider battalions who had landed north of the town had met with success. Their job had been to clear the Germans out of the dropping-zone for the next wave of airborne troops, and it was a very welcome sight indeed when, in the late afternoon, another airborne armada came in, dropping parachutists by thousands. With their arrival, the 6th Airborne Division was all in Germany, ready for the link-up.

With the death of Bill Collins, Charlie Ashton took command of 31 Platoon, which was now about two-thirds normal strength. Major Pearman and Jem Hacker also put in an appearance. By early morning Haminkeln had been turned into a veritable fortress, though with one serious deficiency. We had no anti-tank weapons. Landing as we had done in the middle of a battlefield and coming under fire the moment we hit the ground, there had been no time to unload our hand-carts. So, as soon as dusk began to fall, the major ordered a patrol from each platoon to return to the landing-area to pick up any handcarts and other equipment they could find. As the most experienced corporal, I was duly selected to go and, taking with me Jakoff and Ponsonby, set off. First-aid men followed us to pick up the wounded, who, however, had mostly managed to struggle into the houses dotted along the road. The bodies of the dead, some of whom I recognized and some not, were lying where they had fallen.

It was nearly dark when we reached the field where we had landed. I recognized it by the presence of Bill Collins' body. I noticed that his Browning automatic pistol, binoculars, compass and map were missing, though whether they had been taken by the enemy or by our own troops was impossible to say. I was not going to hang about to investigate. We crossed the field to the point where the glider had landed, but there was nothing left but a heap of charred debris. I suppose that the Germans had guessed there would be ammunition on board and had raked it with machine-gun fire till the ammunition exploded. Obviously our platoon had had little time to spare in leaping free from the glider.

Rather than return empty-handed, I led my small patrol across three or four neighbouring fields, to see if the handcarts of any of the other platoons had survived. Most of the gliders had gone up in flames, but about half a dozen were still reasonably intact. Only one had a handcart in it, however, and that also held its full complement of men. It had been riddled with machine-gun bullets, and the men sat there, still strapped in and all dead.

Despite our familiarity with death, we could not bring ourselves to stumble over the legs of all those dead men to retrieve the handcart, and in any case we would have been very vulnerable to any lurking German patrols. So stealthily we made our way back to town and reported to Charlie Ashton what had happened. No handcart, no PIAT anti-tank mortar and no ammunition. Fortunately there was still no sign of enemy tanks, nor unfortunately, of our ground forces. It was not until I had rejoined my section back in the town that I realized I had not eaten since breakfast that morning and was now extremely hungry. But we had been ordered not to open our emergency twenty-four-hour pack until told to.

My section had been detailed to hold a row of three houses on the outskirts of the town. The front faced the main street, while the rear doors gave a good field of vision over the open Rhineland country. Harry Harris, who had been in charge in my absence, had all the men ostensibly on the look-out, but Tombstone had interpreted that as liberty to indulge in some looting. I soon put a stop to that and told him that, if he wanted to search the houses, he could do so for food. The middle house, which was the biggest of the three, had the table laid, presumably for lunch, but the occupants had as usual disappeared, and so had the food. Eventually Tombstone found some bread and, in a cupboard under the stairs, a veritable hoard of preserved fruit, mostly plums and pears. This will do us, I thought, but I gave priority to making our position safer and called out for that arch-scrounger Tombstone.

"I want some tools," I said, "pickaxes, large hammers, anything like that. We'll knock a hole in the walls on either side, and that'll make it easier for us to maintain contact."

Off he went, to return a few minutes later with a pickaxe, a shovel and a sort of crowbar. Leaving four men on the look-out, two in each direction, I set the other four to work breaking through to the adjoining houses.

I realized there would be no sleep for us that night. Surrounded in enemy territory, we could expect a counter-attack at any time, so our shifts alternated between watching and knocking down those walls. Between times, we managed to get a hasty meal of preserved plums and pears, no doubt bottled by some German *Hausfrau*, together with a chunk of bread, all washed down by hock, of which the inimitable Tombstone had managed to find a couple of bottles. Later we all swallowed our Benzedrine pills, to keep us awake.

At about ten o'clock the platoon runner arrived, asking me to report, with the other section leaders, to Sergeant Ashton.

"I've just come from the major," the sergeant announced. "There's still no news from our land forces. We haven't been able to make contact, because most of our radio sets were lost. However," he continued, "as the other companies have taken their objectives, when they arrive we'll be able to advance over the bridges. But it looks as though this won't be for another twenty-four hours, so make your positions as strong as you can and be ready to move out the morning after next."

I returned to my section with this news, and we set to work fortifying the position by putting furniture against all the doors except one and making ourselves as comfortable as possible for what promised to be a long night. The gunfire to the west seemed to be getting nearer, but within the town there was no sound at all. Everything, including ourselves, was as silent as the grave. We preferred it to stay that way.

Next morning a minor incident occurred which brought home to me the penalties of carelessness. While taking my turn on watch at the front of the house, I suddenly thought of the Walther pistol I had taken from the German officer. So I got it out, loaded the magazine and checked the safety-catch; as I was making myself familiar with it, in case I should ever have occasion to use it, I pressed the trigger, not realizing there was a bullet already up the spout. The sound of the pistol firing in that small front room was like an almighty explosion, and the rest of the section came rushing in to see what was going on. As I explained what had happened, I opened the drawer of the dressing-table near which I had been sitting, and there was a bent and twisted bullet which might well have killed someone. Well, I thought, after coming through all that action yesterday, you could easily have put paid to yourself through one moment of carelessness. It was a salutary lesson.

At the section leaders' conference later that morning, Charlie Ashton had mixed news for us. The good was that the vanguard of the ground forces had made contact with us. The bridgehead over the Rhine was secure, and we were to be prepared to break out within the next forty-eight hours. The bad was that the losses of the Air Landing Brigade, particularly in our battalion, had been the highest ever suffered in any airborne operation. Only one man in three was still in action, so we were told, with the official estimate that the killed, wounded and missing accounted for sixty-seven per cent of our effective strength. D Company had lost about half its men, and 31 Platoon was little better off, while 29 Platoon had very few survivors. It had therefore been decided to amalgamate the two platoons, under the command of Lieutenant Weeks, though it would still be known as 31 Platoon. I wondered how many of the eighteen-year-old lads who had joined D Company with me less than two years ago were still about. Not many, I guessed.

What was it they had said to us at the briefing less than a week ago? Something about the politicians and the public not standing for another Arnhem. Well, those same planners had sent our 6th Air Landing Brigade over a battlefield where many of their gliders were bound to be blown out of the sky. We had been under fire before we had even landed and had suffered enormous casualties. But because we had not been cut off, it was not another Arnhem. The planners could claim a success. Thinking back to the glider full of dead Red Devils, strapped in their seats, I wondered whether they would rather have taken their chances at Arnhem. Our thoughts were very bitter. We would much rather have landed ahead of the assault of the ground forces. "To hell with the armchair planners." We all wished that they could have flown with us.

Another quiet night — no activity from either side, with reports that the Germans were in considerable strength east of Haminkeln and were digging in at the foot of a wooded slope, some half a mile beyond the river. Even though things were quiet, we again took our Benzedrine pills to stay awake; the position was far too precarious to take any chances. My section were still feasting on preserved fruit, some of which we had been able to swop for a whole cheese, but I had to keep insisting that we preserve our emergency rations intact, since we could, if necessary, live on them for several days later on.

After the quiet night, a quiet day, during which some tanks of an armoured brigade came into Haminkeln to join us. Rumour had it that they were going to stay with us for the rest of the campaign, and Lieutenant Weeks told us that there were to be no more trips back to England, to await a call for another airborne landing. From now on, we were to fight as ordinary infantry and, although they had more transport, we Red Devils would be expected to keep up with them, nay ahead of them, even if we had to march all the way. As far as I was concerned, it was just another of the familiar pep talks to which we had to listen from time to time, about our being a *corps d'élite*. It did not cut much ice, but we knew we would do our best when the time came.

What worried me more than the relatively distant future was what would happen within the next day or so, when we had to break out of our bridgehead. As if reading my thoughts, Weeks said that the break-out would be the next morning, and he gave us our orders.

31 and 32 Platoons would lead the way over the river bridge, supported by tanks, and would attack the enemy entrenchments. In order to learn more about the German positions, he intended taking out a patrol that night, and would Corporals Russell and Anderson please volunteer to join him? Jim Russell, who had been with Weeks in Normandy, nodded his willingness. So there was nothing for me to do but to agree as well. Weeks said he had asked me because he knew I had lost my chance of a patrol across the Maas at Blerick. It sounded as though he thought he was doing me a favour. But, with the end of the war approaching, that was the sort of favour I could well do without.

I found the day and the evening dragging interminably. At last, at ten o'clock, I reported to Lieutenant Weeks and found Jim Russell already there. We were wearing steel helmets and flying-smocks with toggle ropes around our waists, and I carried the Schmeisser I had taken from the German officer, in preference to my Sten. Six magazines for it were tucked into the top pockets of my flying-smock, and I had also put the Walther pistol into my belt. I felt like a walking arsenal until I saw that the others were equally heavily armed.

The night was cold and starlit, with faint moonlight. We crept through the silent town and up to the bridge where Weeks gave the password, which was "Bacon and Beans". Yesterday it had been "Ham and Eggs", and on the previous day "Fish and Chips". The sentry said the first word, and the reply was the second. Tomorrow it

179

was to be "Sausage and Mash". The system was simple but effective.

Once over the bridge, we were in no-man's-land. Weeks led the way, then Russell, then myself, across the road which ran parallel to the river and down into a muddy ditch. Once we had become accustomed to the meagre light, we found we had a visibility of thirty or forty yards, which made it imperative that we should not leave the ditch system. So on we went until we could hear the noise of picks and shovels digging in front of us. We halted, and Weeks whispered to me that he and Russell were going to get as near as possible to the enemy lines, to see what was going on and try to form some idea of their numbers.

"Keep a sharp look-out for yourself as well, Corporal," he said, "If we're in trouble, you'll hear firing, then give us covering fire till we get back to help you. If there's no trouble, we'll come back the same way that we're going now. If you don't recognize me, use today's password, but don't speak unless you have to. Finally, if we're not back within an hour, make your own way back and report the enemy position."

We had already synchronized our watches.

"Best of luck," I whispered.

"Hush," breathed Weeks and disappeared.

Within less than a minute I could neither see nor hear them. So I settled down for my lonely vigil, less than two hundred yards from the enemy lines.

Weeks and Russell were back much quicker than I had expected. I had been straining my eyes and ears for any sign of movement but had not yet started looking at my watch because I knew that, if I did, time would go slower and slower. I heard the pair before I could see them. When they drew level I joined them, and without a word we crept back to the road and over the bridge. At Company HQ Russell and I were dismissed by Jem Hacker — naturally without a word of appreciation or encouragement. We left Weeks conferring with the major and other platoon commanders about the best method of attack, in the light of what he had learnt. What that was I never discovered.

At first light the order to attack came. 31 and 32 Platoons, numbering about sixty men in all, crept across the narrow bridge in single file, scarpered over the road and jumped into the ditch. There we spread ourselves out till there were two or three yards between each man. We were stripped for action, to the extent that we had all disposed of any loot we had managed to collect, except I had retained my German dagger and the Walther pistol.

"Fix bayonets," shouted Weeks in the centre of the line. We did so and waited for the word to charge. But it did not come.

Between us and the enemy, dug in at the foot of that wooded slope about half a mile away, were flat, open fields, without a vestige of cover, apart from the ditches which criss-crossed them at right-angles. These ditches were about three feet wide and three feet deep and so would give cover to men on foot. At the same time they would create no problems for the six tanks that were supposed to accompany us. But where were the tanks? None was to be seen. We began to appreciate that this was not good tank country; a tank crossing that flat field would be a sitting duck. Still, it was not going to be a picnic for us, either. After waiting for about fifteen minutes, which seemed like hours to us, crouched in our ditch, one tank, and one only, rumbled over the bridge. This was to be our only support.

It was a Churchill designed for infantry support, but unfortunately we Red Devils had never before fought with tank support. So we proceeded to attack the only way we knew. As the solitary tank crossed the road and plunged into the field, the men on either side opened a gap for it. Then we all climbed out of our ditch and started running forward at top speed, leaving the tank slightly behind us. We had not gone far before we saw puffs of smoke ahead, from the enemy rifles and machine-guns. At this, the gunners in the Churchill fired back with their heavy machine-guns. Meantime, running like mad and zigzagging like frightened rabbits, we gained the first cross ditch. We still had about six hundred yards to go.

"Don't get up in the same place you went down," yelled Weeks, but the men who had stormed Haminkeln had already learnt that lesson. We moved a yard or two to the left or right, then, as the tank caught up with us, off we went again, zigzagging for the next ditch. Men were now beginning to fall, but none of us had time to look to see who they were. We just had to keep going as hard as we could. As we dived into the next ditch, the Churchill's machine-gun was chattering almost non-stop. Four hundred yards to go.

Although we had run so far at top speed, somehow we were not too much out of breath, as we were able to rest for a moment, while our faithful old tank caught up with us. Then we were off again. The enemy fire seemed much heavier now, though miraculously very few men were falling. But there was no time to think.

Run; swerve right; now left; dodge again; keep clear of the tank.

"Come on boys, keep up. Only one more ditch."

In we all dived . . . or nearly all of us. Jack Nichols was hit in the arm a yard short of the ditch. I dragged him in, and he sat in the mud. When he rolled up his sleeve, we could see in his forearm a little red hole, a quarter of an inch in diameter, as neat as the holes that we used to push with our pencils in the targets on the rifle range. He would have to stay where he was. I gave him my sten-gun and took his rifle and bayonet in exchange; they would probably be of more use.

Two hundred yards to go. This was it. This was what it was all about — the endless drilling, marching, training, athletics and discipline. Here we put everything to practical use. The tank stopped. It was not going any farther or it would be within anti-tank mortar range. Still, it had done us proud, though we had uncharitable thoughts about the other five, which we suspected of lurking safely on the far side of the bridge. The bastards!

There was no command. Someone started to climb out of the ditch, and the rest rose with him. I found myself running with all the others towards the German trenches. I could see the Germans plainly now, still firing their rifles. Our tank had stopped firing, for fear of hitting us. There was now no time to swerve or dodge, just run . . . run as fast as your legs could carry you . . . and don't forget to yell and scream at the top of your voice. Never mind if some of your mates were falling or dropping behind. It was now just you or Jerry.

The German trenches were only twenty yards away . . . ten yards . . . five . . . I had picked out my German. Suddenly, it was all over. The Germans were throwing down their arms and raising their hands. They had to be quick; some who were too late got shot. Not one of us had to use a bayonet, but no one, least of all the Germans, had any doubts about our intention of doing so.

In that assault about fifty Red Devils had overwhelmed about twice that number of Germans, after running for about half a mile over open country. We must have been a daunting sight, charging in and yelling, with only a few of us falling. To the enemy we must have looked invincible, and their nerve had broken. As Jem Hacker, who I don't remember seeing there, told the newspaper reporters: "The Germans put up a stiff resistance until we got near enough for them to feel the fear of cold steel going through their bodies, and then they cracked."

Still running, Weeks jumped over the German trenches, with men on either side of him, and entered the wood on the slopes of the hill. There he signalled to us to halt and take cover among the trees. Before we could advance any farther, we would have to wait for the second wave of troops to come up and take charge of the prisoners. As I regained my breath, I looked back over the field and saw the tanks which should have been supporting us now streaming over the grassy plain.

Well, it was nice to know they were around. The first stage of the break-out from the Rhine bridgehead had now been successfully achieved, but with little thanks to the Tank Brigade, save only to our solitary loyal Churchill.

CHAPTER
EIGHTEEN

The Road to Münster

As soon as we had been relieved of our prisoners, we were off again. Weeks signalled to us to advance through the wood, in the face of spasmodic fire from enemy troops somewhere ahead. His idea was, now they were on the run, to press home our advantage, even at the risk of being cut off. A hundred or so yards ahead we could see shadowy figures in field-grey uniforms, dodging between the trees as they retreated. But we had no time to open fire as Weeks kept moving on, and we had as much as we could do to keep up with him.

At the top of the slope the wood came to an end, and about fifty yards ahead we could see a large farmhouse, with a fringe of outbuildings. We were just in time to see the Germans enter the farmyard, the last of them taking refuge in a wooden chicken run.

"Come on," shouted Weeks. "I'll take the house; you go left," he yelled to me, as he led one section away.

As I reached the farmyard, I fired a few rounds into the chicken run and then kicked the door open. Out came two Germans with their hands on their heads. Peering inside, I saw two more lying wounded. I signalled the direction the prisoners were to take, helping the wounded men with them. They seemed somewhat surprised, having evidently been told that the Red Devils did not take prisoners. As soon as it became clear that we did, more Germans appeared from their hiding-places, all eager to surrender. The yard was crowded with British and German, the former rounding up the latter and herding them into the centre.

Typically, Tombstone, always on the scrounge and looking for an excuse to get out of the firing-line, volunteered to march the prisoners back. So did one or two of the older soldiers. Glancing around, I saw wrist watches and rings being removed from German prisoners.

"There's no time for that," I snapped. "Get them back to Number 30 Platoon at the bottom of the slopes and be back here in five minutes. The party's not over yet."

Then Harry Harris called out that he had spotted more Jerries in a large wood, some four hundred yards away, across open fields.

Following Weeks' orders, I led what remained of my section, together with some stragglers, outside the farmyard where we immediately went to ground in long grass under the shadow of the farmyard wall. We were facing the wood, through which we could discern Germans moving cautiously as if they were going to attempt a counter-attack. I ordered my section to open fire in single shots, but, as the minutes ticked on and we saw more and more Germans creeping through the wood, I told them to cease fire. I estimated that we had seen three or four hundred already, and it seemed unwise to draw attention to our position. They would be able to overwhelm us in no time at all.

I called across to Jakoff, the smallest man in our section.

"Get back down the slope to Company HQ and tell them what's happening over there," I told him. "Ask them if they can put down a mortar or artillery barrage. If you can't find Company HQ, keep looking till you find someone in authority. Don't come back till you're satisfied that they've got the message. Tell them that this Jerry counter-attack could be in battalion strength. Keep low, and don't get shot. Our lives are in your hands. The best of luck."

Luck was what Jak had. Just as he reached the bottom of the slope, he came face to face with the colonel, who had brought up reinforcements. The colonel was a man of action. In no time he had formed four three-inch mortars into a battery. They quickly found the range, whereupon the colonel ordered rapid fire. From our vantage-point we could see the results. The mortar shells went crashing in among the trees, doubtless causing many casualties, and before long the Germans, instead of counter-attacking, were in full retreat. I must confess I felt very pleased with myself. It was the first time I had ever been in a position to call for support, and it was gratifying to see it arrive so quickly and so effectively. It was also pleasant to hear the murmurs of "Good old Andy" and "Well done,

Andy" from the men around me. They knew, of course, that it had been a life-or-death matter for all of us.

The Germans did not retreat for long as they found the wood was surrounded. The colonel had got the whole battalion on the move. Whichever way they tried to escape, they would have to cross several hundred yards of open fields. But they had had enough. They surrendered, every one of them, making our bag for that day well over a thousand. Weeks, however, was taking no chances and ordered us to dig in around the farmhouse, which was to be our home for the rest of the day and all night.

It was now early afternoon. We scouted around but found nothing edible in the farm — neither cows, chickes nor any provisions. So, for the first time, we broke into our twenty-four-hour emergency packs. After a lunch consisting of hot soup and hard-tack biscuits, I took Tombstone back through the woods and down the slope towards Company HQ. My section was now very low on ammunition and, as it was too early to expect fresh supplies to be brought up from the rear, I decided that we had better collect all we could from the dead and wounded.

Returning, I did my rounds and saw that everyone was safely dug in. All seemed satisfactory, so I told Harry Harris, my second-in-command, that I was going to take a nap. Half the others could do the same, and then the others, and then we would have two hours on, two hours off, all through the night. It was now six o'clock in the evening, and I thought I would be just

189

about ready for supper when I woke up from my two-hour break.

It was daylight when I awoke. I looked at my watch. Eight o'clock. But eight o'clock the next morning! I had slept for fourteen hours. After more than eighty hours without sleep, once I had curled up in my slit trench I had been lost to the world, and when Harry had been unable to wake me at the end of the first two hours' shift, he had taken charge and reorganized the duty roster so that I could sleep on undisturbed.

"You'd better hurry up if you want any breakfast, Andy," called Harry. "We're due to be moving off again soon."

I hastily made some porridge from the dehydrated cubes, ate it with hard-tack and washed it down with a hot drink made from dehydrated cubes of tea, sugar and milk. I had barely time to get all my gear together before I had to report, with the other section leaders, to Weeks, to get our orders for the day. As an afterthought, I extracted some of the boiled sweets from the pack, to suck on the road; we had been told that they provided energy.

On my return I went over to Harry's slit trench to thank him and the other men for being so considerate. They had even shared the other slit trenches between them so that I could have mine to myself for the night. Much though I appreciated it, I must say I hated to see my reputation for super-fitness and being as hard as nails slipping. I could not escape the feeling that I must have lost face with the men by unconsciously allowing them to pamper me.

"You've carried us along, Andy," said Harry, self-consciously. "It was the least we could do, and the whole section agreed to it."

I could see this was an argument I was not going to win. I felt deeply touched and turned away to hide my embarrassment.

"Come along, all of you," I shouted, more briskly than I needed to. "Let's get moving." They understood my mood and climbed out of their slit trenches, ready to move off.

Looking back, I realized that I had been driving myself hard. We had all of us taken Benzedrine pills to keep awake on the first two nights at Haminkeln, but on the third night the other men had managed to get half a night's sleep, when I was out on patrol. As a result of taking the pills that night as well, I was again unable to get to sleep even when I was back in the town. So perhaps there was the excuse that I needed so much to keep my self-respect!

Now we set off to take over Germany, to advance eastwards into the heart of the Fatherland, with D Company in the lead. Each platoon had now been allocated one Churchill tank in support, which cheered us tremendously as we moved off up the road, towards Berlin.

Although in good spirits, we had no illusions about the way ahead being easy, which was just as well, for only a quarter of a mile along the road we ran into opposition. As machine-guns started firing, we instinctively dived for cover in the ditches. We did not return the fire, for that would have been a waste of ammunition. The Churchills, with their heavy machine-guns and artillery pieces, were there to do that. We simply lay low and let the tanks score direct hits on the farmhouse. By the time the German fire had ceased, the house was reduced to little more than a pile of rubble. Half the upper walls were demolished, and all the doors and windows were blown in.

Weeks led 31 Platoon across the fields to the house at a gallop. We were well spread out and had our bayonets fixed. When we searched the ruined building, however, all we could find, in a sand-bagged enclosure, were the bodies of two men, one with a machine-gun. There was plenty of ammunition left, but the fingers to press the trigger were lifeless. The two Germans in blood-stained SS uniforms had fought and died with the same fatalistic fanaticism that the Japanese kamikaze pilots were displaying on the other side of the globe. It was the first time we had encountered on our advance into Germany this unyielding fanaticism of the SS.

Colonel Charlton had come up by now, to see what was going on. The whole battalion had been delayed by half an hour, and he was not going to have his advance held up by every handful of fanatics that the Germans chose to leave behind. He issued new orders. From now on we were to stick to the road. The tanks were to spread out over the fields on either side and were to shoot up every building as they came to it. Whenever their fire was returned, they were to reduce the building to rubble. The section in the lead were then to see that the place was cleared, while the following troops and tanks would leap-frog past and continue the advance. The enemy were on the run and must be allowed no respite whatsoever. The advance must proceed as quickly as possible, to keep up the pressure.

On and on we went, observing the new tactics. By nightfall we had advanced some fifteen miles. For the night Weeks moved 31 Platoon into a farmyard by the roadside. We were in luck. The farm seemed to be the egg-collecting and packing centre for the area, and Tombstone (who else!) broke into a barn and found thousands and thousands of eggs. There was no other food in the house, but it did not take us long to get a fire going and water boiling in a bucket. We all had hard-boiled eggs for supper that night.

We were now back on the usual routine of two hours on watch, four hours off. Between us we kept the fire going all night, and by morning every man was loaded up with enough hard-boiled eggs to last for several days. It was just as well, for regular rations were still not coming through, and our ration packs were becoming sadly depleted, no matter how sparingly we used them.

During the evening Weeks called together an O Group, which consisted of himself, Charlie Ashton and the three section leaders, Corporals Russell and Robinson and me. Ben Robinson, whom I have not mentioned before, had been drafted into D Company after Normandy and had been in 31 Platoon well before the Battle of the Bulge. He was a tall, thin man in his mid-twenties, a good soldier but not a good mixer. How strange, I thought; this chap's been in the same platoon as me for about six months and yet I hardly know him, even though we have run together in the same cross-country team. Before joining the Airborne Division I had imagined that the Red Devils would be a bunch of raging extroverts, but in fact most of them, particularly the officers and NCOs, were completely the opposite.

My thoughts turned to Weeks, who was talking about the day's activities. He is a strange one, I mused, accepted by neither officers nor men — though probably one of the best subalterns in the whole battalion. Surely after what we had been through together in the past few days we could expect at least to be on Christian-name terms. But no. Indeed, none of us ever did learn what his Christian name was. Though a very brave and dedicated officer, Weeks was a shy and diffident man, never able to let his hair down or even to joke with his NCOs. He was, however, an officer in whom we could have confidence, and we knew he would never ask us to do what he would not do himself.

I recovered from my reverie in time to hear Weeks say that the next day would be very like the one just spent. We would advance through open countryside, on the northern fringe of the Ruhr, the heart of Germany's heavy industry, and with a bit of luck we might even reach Münster tomorrow night. Then on the following night we should be somewhere near the Dortmund-Ems Canal — a name by that time very familiar to listeners to the BBC News as a target, night after night, for the RAF heavy bombers. It was the main waterway between the Ruhr and the North Sea. There were no further orders, except to be ready to move off by eight o'clock sharp the next morning. So, bidding us goodnight, Weeks retired to his own solitary quarters. That quiet, secretive man never shared his digs.

We woke to a breakfast of hard-boiled eggs and had hard-boiled eggs for every meal that day. The major's jeep was now carrying two canisters for each platoon. One was for boiling water and in the sides of the other we had bashed holes. When we stopped for a break, we would fill this second canister with loose earth and then pour petrol, from a jerrican, over it. Set alight, it made a useful portable stove. Then we would wait for the water to boil, not forgetting to use our water-purification sets, and so made tea with some of our dehydrated cubes. It was not tea like mother makes, but it was warm, wet and sweet and helped to wash down the hard-boiled eggs.

All that day we continued our advance over the mainly flat but sometimes undulating North German Plain. Every few miles the leading troops would be held up by small fanatical groups, but the technique of leap-frogging past the defenders was now so familiar to us that dealing with these pockets of enemy resistance was routine. Although we were on foot, we were going forward at a rate of approximately fifteen miles a day, towing our handcarts with us.

The wheels of our handcarts, though, were now not the only wheels we had. As we passed along the road, we commandeered every means of transport we could find. Private cars were borrowed till they ran out of fuel. Quite a few men had taken bicycles out of houses, and even children's scooters and prams were being pressed into service. Anything that could take some of the loads we had to carry was worth requisitioning. Harry Harris, with his mates Alfie Ross and Ray Best, now had an armoured perambulator as their Bren-gun carrier. It carried not only the gun but also tins of food and bottles of preserved fruit, looted from houses along the road, together with hundreds of rounds of .303 ammunition.

To the German civilians we must have presented an alarming spectacle as we plodded on with our ramshackle vehicles. We were gaunt, dirty and unshaven, the natural result of sleeping rough and eating whenever we had a chance. One or two of our officers were now riding horses, and as I was giving a hand to Harry with his armoured pram, I thought, with a grin, that we must look more like a retreat from Moscow than a victorious army on the march. Still, no doubt the German civilians, peeping from their hide-outs, must have concluded that, if this ragamuffin army could defeat their own crack troops, we must be indeed Red Devils. It did us no harm for them to think so.

Although we had no official transport, reports being received from other sectors, where the Infantry Divisions were well supplied with transport, showed us that the Sixth Airborne Division was keeping pace with the rest of the army. But the strain was beginning to tell.

One evening, when 31 Platoon was again in the lead, our advance was stopped at dusk. We curled up in ditches on either side of the road and slept, leaving guards posted on a two-hour-on, four-hours-off shift. In the pale moonlight along came an elderly German corporal on a bike. We could see he was not armed and therefore represented no danger, so we let him pass. Some of the men were too tired to notice, while the sentry and myself thought it a great joke, as the German was evidently quite unaware of our presence. The poor chap rode his unlit bike confidently into our Company HQ. He did not get past Jem Hacker, though, who happened to be on the alert and who did not have much sense of humour. We reckoned the German must have been the only prisoner the sergeant-major had ever taken by himself, and we had a good laugh about it next day. We would have given a lot to have seen the German's face when he discovered where he was.

We did not laugh that night, though, when the sergeant-major turned up with Major Pearman and gave us, and particularly me, a good rollicking for letting the German pass.

"You'll be on a charge for this, Corporal," barked Hacker.

"I'm sorry," I said, "but I let him through as I didn't know whether there were any more following him, and I didn't want to give our positions away."

It was a lie, of course, but it got me out of trouble.

"Quite right, Corporal," said the major, and that was the end of the episode.

Meantime, our battalion had now been allotted three jeeps manned by the SAS, in addition to our tanks. The

Special Air Service were the élite of the élite, even compared with the Red Devils. In action they were dropped miles ahead of the rest of the division, together with their specially equipped jeeps. These was partially armoured, carried a crew of three and were armed with two sets of twin-mounted light machine-guns at roof level. The SAS, who wore the conventional airborne outfit and red beret, were to advance eastwards at high speed, keeping in constant radio contact with Battalion HQ. Their task was to reconnoitre the country ahead and spot road blocks and other defences that were likely to hold up the main advance. Often they would charge through the obstacles at high speed in order to turn around and attack them from the rear or to give covering fire from the flank for us involved in the frontal attack.

It was the SAS attached to our battalion who were the first British troops to arrive in Münster, our next objective. They reported back that the town was undefended. This was rather surprising, because the town had been heavily bombed, and the ruined buildings and piles of rubble would have made an ideal defensive position. As it was, we were able to march through the northern suburbs without the rattle of machine-gun and sniper fire about our ears and into a town where from the window of every building left standing there hung the white flag of surrender, in the form of a bed sheet or tablecloth..

For us Münster provided the first evidence we had seen of the devastation caused by Allied bombing. I was quite familiar with the appearance of bombed London but, compared with London, Münster was appalling. Beyond street upon street of ruined or badly damaged houses were other areas, many acres of them, where the whole town had been bulldozed away. They were just seas of rubble. Even the men from the worst-bombed British cities were shaken, and we found ourselves feeling sorry for the German civilians, despite our training that taught us to regard them as enemies.

Later, after we had bypassed the northern part of the town, the SS took over the control of the ruins and proceeded to defend them vigorously. Several British units spent a very nasty four days, clearing the town street by street. However, we were now some miles ahead and continuing our march eastwards.

CHAPTER NINETEEN

The Hitler Youth Fanatics

The effect of the bombing on the civilian population of Germany was much the same as on the civilians in British cities. Far from battering them into submission, it strengthened their resolution. We met frequent examples of defiance.

An early one was from the owner of a house outside Münster which we proposed commandeering for the night. Taking Jakoff with me, I knocked at the door. After a considerable time it was opened by an old lady who must have been seventy if she was a day. She stood barring the doorway and brandishing a broom. I had brought Jakoff because, being of Jewish descent, he could speak Yiddish and had told me that the similarity of the language made it possible for him to understand German. The old girl hurled what was evidently a stream of abuse at us, and I began to get annoyed.

"What's the old girl on about, Jak?" I enquired.

Jak explained, with a grin. "She says, our boys are still in the area, and they've promised to be back, and they will."

"You tell her they won't," I replied. "Tell her the war's as good as over." I waited for him to relay the message. "And tell her, too, that we're taking over her house for the night, and providing she makes no trouble, we won't hurt her or take her food."

Again I waited for Jak to repeat the message, then, pushing past the old woman, I entered the house. Having inspected it, I decided that the old lady could stay on the ground floor, while the six of us would occupy two rooms on the first floor, since windows commanded the street in both directions.

We quickly unloaded the pram and carried our gear up the stairs. I noticed the old woman eyeing the food as we brought it in and told Jak to enquire whether she had any in the house and found that she had not. Although we were under strict instructions not to fraternize, we could not see the old lady starve. So Jak gave her two tins of meat. We did not expect it to make any change in her attitude, and we were right. Next morning, as we left the house, she was still shouting abuse at us. We laughed, and Jak interpreted the gist of her remarks.

"You can laugh now, but you won't be laughing when our boys come back."

Our next objective was the large town of Osnabrück, some thirty-five miles north-east of Münster. All day long our motley gang of invaders marched on over the German plain. We left behind us a trail of destruction wherever resistance was encountered, and often barns, houses and hayricks were fired as a precaution, lest they should hold lurking enemy. Now and again we came up against a road-block, when the leading company was left to deal with it while the rest of the battalion made a detour of a mile or two across open country. By nightfall we arrived at the line of the Dortmund-Ems Canal.

The night was overcast and black as a coal-cellar, as we crept up the bank and looked down at the water, many feet below. As our eyes became accustomed to the darkness, we could make out the dim steel framework of the bridge's superstructure. Following it along, we could just discern a point where it had been blown up and tilted at a crazy angle down to the water.

Major Pearman ordered a flare to be fired. By its light we could see that parts of the superstructure were projecting above the surface of the water. It would be possible to clamber across. The flare also warned the enemy, who were lining the far bank, that we had arrived, and they opened up with everything they had. Soon a battle was raging across the canal, there about fifty yards wide, and it looked as though we were going to be stuck there until daylight, when the colonel appeared.

"We've got to get across tonight," he announced, calmly and without hesitation. "We can't wait until daylight, and anyhow we would probably lose more men."

The sloping bank on our side up which we had climbed to answer the enemy fire was about six feet high. Studying it, he said to Major Pearman, "If I get the tanks up here, two or three on either side of the bridge but below the top of the bank, they could use

202

their guns to make Jerry keep his head down. I'll make sure that they don't fire on the bridge itself. Then your company can clamber over the bridge and make their assault up the roadway on the other side."

The major nodded.

"Weeks," he said, "you will lead with your platoon."

"Very good, sir," said Weeks.

The colonel went away, and within a few minutes we could hear the tanks moving into position. We got out of their way and began to congregate around the abutment to the bridge.

The colonel was back.

"As soon as D Company are over," he promised, "A Company will follow, and then the others. If things go well, we could have the whole battalion across within two hours, as Jerry can't have that many troops over there." As an after-thought he added, "It'll mean leaving the tanks behind, once we're over, but I dare say they'll catch up again in a day or two."

Weeks reported, "All ready to move off, sir. When we get across, I'll move right along the bank, and Lieutenant Black, of Thirty Platoon, will move left."

"Good man," said the colonel. Then, addressing them both, he concluded, "When you get across, fire your Very pistols to show your progress along the banks, so that the tanks can keep their fire well in front of you. We don't want to shoot our own men. Good luck."

At a signal, all the tanks opened up with their machineguns, and we could see, too, the tracer bullets darting across the canal. A tracer bullet leaves a red streak as it passes along its trajectory, thus enabling the machine-gunners to check the accuracy of their fire. The tanks were allowing about six feet clearance on either side of the bridge and now and again, just for good measure, would fire their seventy-five-millimetre guns. The enemy's fire died away.

Weeks went down the roadway and onto the bridge, followed by the rest of us in single file. Suddenly the sky lit up. The Jerries had put up a parachute flare, and everyone already on the bridge froze against the steel girders of the superstructure. Then one of the tank gunners showed great initiative as his tracer bullets went arching upwards, almost immediately hitting the flare, which fell down and sizzled to extinction in the canal.

We started moving forward again, and most of us were nearing the other bank before the next flare went up. Some, however, were still on the steelwork when the Germans opened up again with their machine-guns. In the garish light I saw two men hit and fall into the water, but as the flare died out, Weeks yelled across to Black, "Let's go before they put up another flare." Up the bank he charged, followed by about thirty men. On reaching the top we turned at right angles and advanced along the canal bank. The Germans now under fire from their flanks as well as the front retreated into the night, leaving a number of wounded behind.

We deployed ourselves fanwise around our little bridgehead and, as we dug in for the night, I recalled the strange feeling I had when crossing the canal in the pitch blackness. It was as though I was moving not into the heart of Germany but into the depths of hell, or somewhere very evil. I said as much next day to several of my men, who claimed to have experienced much the same feeling, as though someone were walking over their graves.

Not only our tanks but all our other transport, orthodox and otherwise, had to be left on the west bank of the canal, when we marched next morning in the general direction of Osnabrück. Ahead we could see a range of wooded hills known as the Teutoburgerwald, the only hills of any height in the whole of the North German Plain and where the enemy, having failed to hold the line of the Dortmund-Ems Canal, could be expected to make a further stand. It seemed likely that the next little town, Lengerich, from where both roads and railway led through the hills to Osnabrück, would be defended, and just before we arrived there we learnt that the engineers had managed to put a Bailey bridge across the canal. Our SAS jeeps and two armoured scout cars came over and caught up with us, bearing the welcome news that the tanks would soon be following.

The first sign of the German defence of Lengerich was a direct hit on one of the armoured scout cars. Only one man managed to bale out. Immediately three companies deployed for the attack while the fourth was despatched to capture and hold a long wooded ridge that overlooked the town. By mid-afternoon, strengthened by the arrival of the tanks, we had broken through the main defences and were entering the town, where the colonel gave each of us a sector to clear. The men of the company looking down on us from their wooded ridge must have thought they were well out of danger. They were soon to learn otherwise.

Lengerich was only a small place, of a few thousand inhabitants, but it was not until nightfall that the last enemy shot was fired. If, on looking back through my period of active service, I were to be asked what was the worst day I had experienced, I would have to admit, "That day in Lengerich."

Though the Germans were outnumbered, they defended the town, street by street, house by house, floor by floor, even room by room. Whereas in previous street fighting it had been a matter of locating the enemy and forcing him out, this time we were engaged with opponents of fanatical tenacity.

Most of the civilians were in the cellars. With Jakoff as my interpreter, we dealt with them curtly but not unkindly. We warned them that for a civilian to be found carrying arms was an offence for which he could be shot. Fortunately they seemed to be already aware of that and gave us no trouble.

We cleared the streets of Lengerich in our practised tactics, and as we neared the town centre, we sensed, rather than heard or saw, that the enemy were retreating ahead of us. When we reached the last house, we guessed that, as we had not caught up with them, the last of them must have holed up there. It was my turn to clear this house. We could not throw in any grenades first, as we had long ago exhausted our supplies, so we charged into the ground floor, with bayonets at the ready. It was empty. The Germans were upstairs.

The house was only a small one — two rooms up and two down. I guessed that, to escape from the covering fire from our men across the road, the Jerries must be in the rear bedroom. So, just to be on the safe side, I got Alfie Ross to fire a magazine of his Bren-gun up through the ceiling, spraying his fire all over the room. Then Alfie, Ray Best and I charged up the stairs, while Tombstone, Ponsonby and Jakoff dashed into the back garden and started firing into the upstairs window. Standing well back on the landing, I let Alfie fire another magazine through the door before I kicked it open. After a pause, out came one German with his hands on his head. Another was sitting on the floor wounded, while a third was lying dead in the front bedroom. They did not have a single round of ammunition left between them but refused to surrender until the bitter end. After having steeled ourselves for close-quarter combat, it was a bit of an anticlimax.

As we brought our prisoners from the house, we were intrigued to see, in the deepening dusk, four Germans run out of the last house across the square and try to start up the colonel's jeep. Before we could open fire, the colonel himself dashed out of another house, shot two of them with his revolver, at fifteen yards range, and took the other two prisoners. Those were the last shots heard in the town that night. Lengerich had finally fallen.

We made ourselves as comfortable as we could and ate our first meal since breakfast. Throughout the night we could hear spasmodic firing from the direction of the wooded ridge which the fourth company was holding. The next morning the news was grim. During the evening and night they had lost twenty-six men killed and wounded by snipers. The colonel was furious and was not going to let the Jerries get away with that. At first light, leaving one company to control the town, he took the remainder of the battalion up to the wooded hill. There we formed a line and swept the wood from end to end, killing half a dozen snipers and capturing four others, who were marched down to the town. In the school where the colonel had set up Battalion HQ, he inspected their rifles, which were fitted with telescopic sights. Then he ordered them to be stood against the playground wall and shot.

I was able to take a good look at the prisoners. They were blond, fresh-faced boys, dressed in the uniform of the Hitler Youth. The oldest could not have been more than sixteen, and the youngest probably only fourteen. They knew they were going to be shot and admitted that they were aware of the penalty beforehand and were prepared to die. Their faces were hard, grim and sullen, without a trace of remorse. A firing-squad was formed from the company which had suffered so grievously at the hands of the snipers, and as I went back to my billet, I heard the volley. Mingled with my compassion for the boys who had died so young was hatred for the evil men who had brainwashed them and trained them to kill, when, in normal circumstances, they should have still been at school.

Immediately after lunch the order came to move on. We heard this without regret. None of us was sorry to leave Lengerich.

"If every town is going to be defended like this one," I remarked, "this war's going to take a long time to finish."

Osnabrück was some ten miles away to the north, and we reached it in the early evening after only minor skirmishes and were relieved to find that it was undefended. It had been badly battered by Allied bombers, though, as in Münster, the cathedral and the Peace Hall stood almost intact. It seemed to me incongruous that in such a warlike country as Germany the two big towns we had seen so far should each have a Peace Hall.

The night was uneventful, and next morning we were off again, marching eastwards. As we went, we began to collect an assortment of vehicles similar to those we had had to abandon at the Dortmund-Ems Canal. So we went on, day after day, and on 4th April arrived on the west bank of the River Weser, about ten miles north of Minden, where the battle was fought in 1759 during which some of the British regiments stuck roses in their hats as they went forward to attack the French. All that I knew about the River Weser was that it was where the Pied Piper of Hamelin led all but one of the town children to be drowned. Some lines from the poem, parts of which I had learned at school, ran through my mind. I little realized that the next group to be led away by the banks of the Weser would include myself.

We camped for the night on the bank of the river. As we gazed down at the swift-flowing water, Frank Ponsonby quoted, incorrectly though aptly,

The River Weser fast and wide,
With German tanks on the other side.

Not only was the River Weser fast and wide, but Air Reconnaissance had reported that all bridges had been blown. This time we saw no hope of crossing that night but were told that collapsible canvas boats would be available next morning. The news filled me with no sort of elation at all. I had already been in a canvas boat in the middle of a river, with enemy troops gunning for me, and I was not looking forward to a repetition of the experience.

On patrol that night I reviewed our progress so far with a certain pride and satisfaction. We had now been in Germany for twelve days and had foot-slogged nearly 150 miles, not far short of 20 miles a day when advancing. We had been heavily laden with equipment and had had to fight frequent battles and skirmishes, which though spasmodic, were often fierce. We were the first British troops to reach the Weser, and tomorrow we would be the first ones across.

I was in one of the first three boats to cross while the rest of the company were ready to give covering fire. But it was not necessary. Some Germans whom we had seen moving along the bank on the previous evening had vanished. We crossed, kneeling in our boats and paddling Red Indian fashion, without incident. It was a tremendous relief to land on the other bank, without once coming under fire. The empty boats were then pulled back by cables which we had made from the five-foot lengths of toggle rope carried by every man. They had a loop at one end and a wooden toggle at the other and were therefore easily joined together.

We deployed ourselves fanwise around a small beach on the river bank, and I found myself in a ditch with Tombstone. We were facing east, with our rifles at the ready, when I spotted a man leave a farmhouse about a quarter of a mile away and start to run towards us waving a white flag. I got the man in my sights, and the temptation to squeeze the trigger and see the body collapse was so overwhelming that Tombstone had to shout at me.

"Don't shoot, Andy. He's carrying a white flag."

"I didn't notice it till you told me," I lied.

Tombstone gave me a queer look. He understood.

Weeks through Jak interrogated the German and was told that the German troops had gone and that he was in the farmhouse on his own, having sent his family away. He had come out into the open hoping to save his house from being burnt down.

I was to wish later that I had squeezed the trigger.

Within an hour the whole company was across, minus the three-inch mortar teams and all our transport and, of course, Percy Pearman and Jem Hacker. From now on, until the Royal Engineers bridged the river, everything, including the PIAT mortar and bombs, had to be carried by hand. The order was given to "advance to contact". This meant that we had to go forward, along the road which we had now reached, until we made contact with the enemy.

"This is fine," I thought. "Here we are, the only British troops east of the Weser. We've got no tanks, armoured cars, jeeps, artillery, anti-tank guns or any transport, and behind us there's not a single bridge standing." I felt almost as if I were undressed as we swung along the road.

The first village, now in sight, was three or four miles from the river, and as we approached it, no shots were fired. The German civilian whom I had so nearly shot was apparently right: the enemy troops had withdrawn. It lent support to the rumour, now widely current, that Hitler had decided to concentrate his armies around a "southern redoubt" somewhere in the Bavarian Alps. That would have suited us very well, as long as we were not selected to attack the redoubt, though past experience suggested that we would inevitably be in the lead.

The front half of the company were already in the village, and we in the rear half were still advancing, in Indian file strung out on either side of the road, when we came under fire. At the same moment there came a loud, mechanical roar that sounded just like a tank engine starting up. It was followed by a massive rumbling of tracks, and from their hiding-places in the village five German tanks appeared. Four of them were giant Tigers, and the fifth was a Mark 4. 31 Platoon was trapped in flat, open countryside, without even the cover of houses to fight from. Our only anti-tank weapon was Ted Lockey's Piat mortar, its eight bombs carried by various members of the platoon. We had walked into a perfectly sprung ambush. Damn that German civilian.

"Get all the Piat bombs to Lockey, and then take cover in the slit trenches," yelled Weeks.

The slit trenches had been dug by the Germans, probably for the benefit of lorry drivers when attacked by our Air Forces. Now they would serve us. I dashed around, collected all the bombs and got them to Ted Lockey before dropping into the nearest trench. Tombstone was there already. We crouched as low as we could, as the tanks rumbled down the road towards us. The PIAT mortar, we had been taught, was capable of knocking out any known tank. Now we would see.

As the first Tiger came within fifty yards, Weeks ordered Lockey to fire. Ted scored a direct hit, and the tank stopped. The engine faded out, and we were jubilant, preparing to take on the tank crews with small arms. Suddenly the engine started up again, and the monster began to lumber forward. Ted Lockey hit the same tank seven more times, but it came remorselessly on. That was the last of our PIAT ammunition. We had nothing but rifles and bayonets.

With no more bombs being fired at them, the Panzers now slewed across the road into the fields and began shooting us up in our slit trenches. We kept our heads down — there was no point in putting your head up to fire a rifle at a sixty-ton tank. On the other hand, the tank crews were not going to show themselves for fear of getting shot, so they lowered their sights as far as possible and tried to kill us in our trenches. But they could not get low enough. In the end they won the completely uneven contest by sheer weight. As the giant tanks towered over the trenches, the soil started to crumble and bury the occupants. One by one 31 Platoon was forced to surrender. Among them was Tombstone, who climbed out of the slit trench he shared with me and held up his hands. But I stayed where I was.

Lying in the bottom of the trench, I buried the German flag I had captured in Haminkeln and the German officer's Walther pistol and SS dagger in loose earth at the bottom of the trench. Then I lay low and waited, hoping I would not be noticed. I thought I had a chance, as the German crews were, quite sensibly, still not prepared to leave their tanks.

The sound of rumblings increased, and I could feel vibrations at the bottom of my trench as the tanks started to move off. The column of captured Red Devils was near enough for me to see them as they were being marched away, along the side of the road. Unfortunately, as they passed my trench, they all leaned over and glanced down, presumably to say a last farewell, thinking I was dead.

Their action did not pass unnoticed. The last tank in the column stopped. The tank commander climbed down, walked across to my trench and, leaning over, pointed a Luger pistol at me. In perfect English he said, "For you, the war is over."

CHAPTER
TWENTY

"For You the War is Over!"

Even in that moment of fear I remember that the officer's words struck me as being slightly ludicrous — on a par with the alleged words of H. M. Stanley when he met David Livingstone in Central Africa: "Dr Livingstone, I presume" — "For you the war is over!"

It was the classic statement of capture, almost a cliché. I looked into the eyes of this handsome, fair-haired, intelligent-looking German officer and saw that he had no intention of shooting me. He had the stamp of an officer and a gentleman of the old school.

He motioned me to climb out of the trench, which I did, leaving my rifle and bayonet behind. Then I walked over to my comrades, where I also abandoned my steel helmet and the rest of my military equipment as they had done. We were marched towards the village in our flying-smocks and red berets. I was still feeling very annoyed with the men of my platoon for revealing my hiding-place, and I told them so in no uncertain manner. Still, their only real fault was that they had not thought quickly enough. There was nothing to be done about it now; we were all prisoners.

As our column came level with a hedgerow some fifty yards short of the village, Harry Harris, probably the best quarter-miler in the company, made a dash for freedom. He had not covered more than thirty yards before one of the tanks opened up on him with a machine-gun. We could see the bullets hitting the ground all around him as he ran. For a few moments he seemed to bear a charmed life, then he was beyond a hedge and out of our range of vision. We never learnt whether he got away or not, but I could not see how anyone could escape being hit by such intense fire at such short range. Anyway, the Germans never went back for him. It was a brave dash but a saddening experience, for Harry had been a good soldier, a staunch friend, and we had gone through a lot together.

The tanks stopped in the village square, keeping us covered while one man from each tank got out and searched us for further arms. They found nothing. None of us felt like doing anything so rash as concealing arms at this stage of the war.

I looked around to see whether many of our number were unaccounted for, but the Germans had made a thorough job of it. They had rounded up most of us. Their tank ambush had completed what had begun at Breville and continued at the Battle of the Bulge and the Rhine Crossing, namely the decimation of D Company. Of the hundred or so eighteen-year-olds who had involuntarily volunteered to join the Red Devils less than two years earlier (though it seemed like two centuries), there could not have been as many as twenty still free and bearing arms. They, presumably, were hiding somewhere in the village, powerless to make any attempt to rescue us. D Company had ceased to exist as a fighting unit. It was a saddening thought, but more than once I had had the premonition that we were not destined to see the end of the war together. One experiences such intense feeling and convictions in times of great stress and effort.

The German officer who had taken me prisoner proved to be the commander of the tank squadron, and when the search was over, he stood up in his turret and made a speech.

"Your country and my country should be friends," he said in faultless English. "We should not be fighting on opposite sides; instead, we should both be fighting together against the threat of World Communism."

No sooner had he finished than out of the western sky swooped a flight of Tiffies. Probably one of the survivors of D Company, hidden somewhere in the village, had managed to get a radio call through to HQ. During this diversion Weeks managed to escape, but before any of the others could follow, the tanks turned their guns on us. The officer's face changed. He was no longer the smiling gentleman but a commander anxious about the safety of his tanks.

"If your Air Force want our tanks, they will have to shoot you as well," he said.

In response to his rapid orders we were forced at gunpoint to climb onto the giant Tigers and a moment later were more than grateful to the man who first suggested that airborne troops should wear such distinctive headgear as a red beret. On their second swoop the Tiffie pilots evidently saw us. They waggled their wings and disappeared, doubtless thinking that the Red Devils had captured the tanks and not vice versa.

The German officer must have sent a message to the local area commander, for presently six armed guards arrived to escort us to a prisoner-of-war camp at Fallingbostel, about thirty miles north of Hanover and some fifty miles from our present location. Whether it was a prisoner-of-war camp or a concentration camp we did not know, and anyhow the truth about the concentration camps was not then fully known. But rumours about what went on there were enough to worry Jakoff, who by descent was a Russian Jew. He told me frankly that he did not fancy his chances of survival once he got inside any kind of German camp and that at the first opportunity he was going to try to escape. Jak had already told Frank Ponsonby, who was also keen on the idea, and when he mentioned it to me, I saw that my best chance would be with Jakoff, who knew the language. So I agreed to join them and was immediately elected leader of the party.

We set off on foot but, with six guards armed with rifles, escape was out of the question until the odds improved. However, the guards seemed in no hurry, and we certainly were not, so we just dawdled along. I reckoned that, at the rate we were moving, it would take us four or five days to arrive at the camp, and that suited us very well. The longer we were on the road, the better the odds in favour of our escaping. At the same time, I told Jak and Frank they must be on the look-out for any opportunity and be ready to take it at a moment's notice.

One of the guards was a Stalingrad veteran who was minus an arm. Two more were in their forties and had been sent home from the Russian Front with slight wounds. The other three must have been in their fifties and seemed to be members of the German Home Guard. The one-armed man, who was about my age, was a corporal and was wearing one of the grades of the Iron Cross. He had slung across his chest a Schmeisser sub-machine-gun which he could use one-handed, while all the others carried the standard Mauser rifles. There appeared to be no chance of any of them looking the other way while we escaped. On the other hand, they were not out for trouble and were inclined to be lenient as long as we did as we were told.

All this information and more Jak gleaned on our easy-paced journey north-eastwards. He soon knew their life-histories and war experiences and that they were worried by the Russians. The corporal told Jak he had lost his arm when escaping from Stalingrad, where he had seen German prisoners have their heads split open with machetes and straw stuffed into their brains. They all hoped that, if they were to be captured, it would be by the British or Americans, not by the Russians. But they were not as yet convinced that the war was lost and thought that the Führer had more secret weapons up his sleeve. Their blind faith in their leader was still not completely shaken.

Jak had all the typical Jewish cockney bubbling wit and cheekiness, which he used during the march to keep up his dialogue with the guards. His particular friend, apparently the best informed, who must have been near sixty, used to get tired towards the end of the day's march. Tombstone bet Jak he could not persuade the fellow to let Jak carry his rifle, and Jak accepted the wager. After about an hour of using his persuasive tongue, there was Jak carrying the rifle! He could have sold snow to an Eskimo. However, he quickly handed the weapon back when the young Stalingrad veteran came running up ready to use his Schmeisser.

It was just as typical of Tombstone to make the bet as it was to decline to join us in our escape bid. I was disappointed for he had become my right-hand man, but Tombstone was always the one to take a soft option when offered.

During the march I thought a good deal about the ethics of being a prisoner of war. We had been taught that Red Devils should never surrender, at least while they had ammunition, but, on the other hand, we were also told there was no point in throwing one's life away. It had been made clear that, if taken prisoner, our first duty was to escape, and we had been fully briefed on that subject. I felt keenly the humiliation of being a prisoner. It went badly against the grain to stand with my hands on my head while strangers searched me. On the other hand, I had not been robbed of my watch, money and personal belongings as I had seen happen to German prisoners. I resented being forced at gun-point to climb on the tank when the Tiffies attacked, but I knew that, in similar circumstances, the Red Devils would have done the same thing.

My worst humiliation was in a small town near Hanover where we halted with the prisoners in the roadway and the guards on either pavement. For no reason that I could think of, then or afterwards, I stepped onto the pavement. At that moment along came an elderly German, bearing himself like an old-time Prussian general. He pushed me off into the rain-filled gutter. I turned to protest, only to have the old man spit straight in my face. This was more than I could stand, but as I moved forward to hit him, several of my companions caught hold of me and hauled me back into their midst. By the time the guards arrived and started to question the old warrior, he was unable to identify the red-bereted soldier who was going to attack him.

The first two nights on the march we were locked in barns, where we slept in the hay, while the guards took turn and turn about outside. The only food we were given was small bowls of weak vegetable soup with a chunk of black bread, night and morning. During the day we stopped at mealtimes, out of force of habit, but received nothing to eat or drink, and the only other food we had was our canned bars of concentrated chocolate. By the third day all had gone, no matter how sparingly we tried to eke it out. The guards themselves fared no better, and some of the prisoners shared their chocolate with the Germans, washing it down with water from roadside streams. We walked as slowly as possible in the hope that British troops would catch up

221

with us but were not very confident, for we knew that, until the Weser was bridged and a strong tank force got across, those Panzers who had captured us, and others like them, could hold up any number of unsupported infantry.

Our first real ray of hope came on the third day, when a party of about fifty Polish slave workers, escorted by two guards, joined the column. That made eight guards to keep an eye on over eighty men, which certainly seemed better odds. However, the countryside was flat and open, with very little cover.

Naturally the talk of escape spread until everyone knew of our intention. We had no further volunteers to join us, but when the column halted for the night, Captain O'Neil, D Company second-in-command, called me to one side and, to my amazement, said, "Corporal, you must stop this silly talk of escape."

"It's not silly talk," I retorted hotly. "It's the duty of every prisoner of war to escape, and we're only doing our duty as soldiers."

"Now look here, Corporal," O'Neil almost shouted, "prisoner or not, I'm the senior officer here, and I forbid any more talk of escape. It's only upsetting the men, and if the guards know what's going on, they're liable to shoot us all."

I looked at O'Neil. To hell with rank, I thought.

"If we want to escape, we will, and there's nothing you can do to prevent it," I said, sharply.

O'Neil backed down. "I didn't say you couldn't escape, but keep your plans to yourself and don't upset the other men," he retorted, as he strode away.

While this conversation was going on, the prisoners and the Poles were being herded into barns and locked up for the night, but I could see that the captain had been talking to the other men, for we three tended to be ostracized. Lieutenant Black, however, was holding an earnest whispered conversation with Jak, and when he had finished, he hung around while Jak had a word with Frank and me.

"Blackie wants to escape with us," said Jak. "He's Jewish, you know." Frank and I looked around at Black.

"Well, I'd never have guessed it," said Frank.

"That's why he wants to escape. He's in the same boat as I am, and the Germans would soon find out he's a Jew."

"I hardly know the man," I objected. "He's seen next to no action. I'm not at all happy putting myself in his hands."

"Not necessary," replied Jak. "He wants to join our escape party, and he says he'll be pleased to accept you as leader."

"Thanks very much," I retorted dryly. "Still, I suppose one more won't hurt, and, as nobody else had asked, I think we can take him. What say you, Frank?"

"It's OK with me," was Frank's immediate response.

So Jak gave Black the thumbs-up sign, and off he went to join O'Neil in the officers' corner. When we set off next morning, we found Black walking alongside us, though no words were exchanged on the now-taboo subject.

During the lunchtime break we were joined by yet another column of prisoners. These were more slave labourers and included Poles, Russians and some Czechs, as far as Jak could make out. His Yiddish seemed to be a universal Eastern European language. These prisoners were in a terrible state; they were dishevelled and clad in extremely dirty clothing and were arguing about what appeared to be handfuls of lentils and some roots they had managed to grub out of the fields. Still, their arrival meant that the odds were steadily improving, as we were now two or three hundred prisoners with less than twenty guards. On the other hand, Fallingbostel could not be more than one day's march away, a fact which Jak was able to confirm in conversation with the guards.

Up to now the signposts on roads that led to the right had all been marked "Hanover", but now Hanover was behind us, and the signposts to the right were marked "Celle". I thought this might be a good omen, as at Celles in the Ardennes we had been free.

The countryside was becoming more wooded, offering good cover for escape. It would have to be this afternoon or never, I thought. Certainly we must try before the evening halt. I passed the message to the others.

The airborne troops were nearly in the middle of the long column, and we four were at the rear of this contingent. As we were the star prisoners, our original guards still kept fairly close to us, but they also had to take their share of guard duty on the whole column. At about four in the afternoon we were walking slowly along the road through a large wood when we spotted a sharp bend to the right, about two hundred yards ahead.

"This is it," I whispered. "Right on the bend."

That was all that was necessary. The others understood. The moment we reached the bend, I ran like mad, jumped a ditch and, zigzagging from side to side, made for the wood. The others followed. A few rifle shots crashed into the wood, but the guards were in a dilemma, as we had hoped. They had to make up their minds whether to give chase or stay with the column. Naturally they chose the latter. What were four prisoners out of several hundred? Anyway, they thought we had no food and no maps, so we could not get far.

I continued running for about four hundred yards, swerving among the trees. Then, stopping to allow the others to catch up with me, I looked back to see if there was any pursuit.

There was none. We were free.

CHAPTER
TWENTY-ONE

Tables Turned

We were fortunate enough to have fine weather for our escape. That was about the only item on the credit side of our situation. Here were we four, in a strange and hostile country with no food, no arms, not even a knife. After making sure that we were not being followed, I tore open the stitching of my battledress and extricated the map concealed there, but the scale was too small to be of any use. I also tried to use the compass composed of those two specially prepared brass buttons, but the direction it indicated as north was different from what it should have been according to the sun.

"What next?" asked Black.

I thought for a moment. We did not have a plan, except to make our way westwards.

"We don't really know the direction we've been marching in since we've been prisoners," I pointed out. "It could have been due east, or south-east, or north-east. I think the only safe course is to head due west. It's now just after four o'clock, so if we head slightly to the right of the sun for the next couple of hours and then into the sun, we should be on the right course to get back to our own lines ... though goodness knows what unit it'll be."

After about two hours we left the forest and were in open country. Keeping due west became more difficult, as we had to stay away from roads and tracks and to keep, as far as possible, to hedges and ditches. So our westward course was decidedly zigzag.

Only once did we see a human being, and that was a German soldier with a rifle slung over his soldier, wheeling a bicycle along a road possibly on some sort of patrol. We all hid in a ditch as he approached and walked within five yards. It was a long, straight road, and after he had passed, it was going to be quite a time before he was out of sight. So, becoming impatient, one by one we scampered across the road. Some instinct caused the German to half-turn, and he did so just as Jak was running across. The German hesitated, and we all held our breath. Then he turned and resumed his patrol, evidently disinclined to make an effort to find us, so we continued our way and presently found ourselves in another dense wood. In a clearing was a solitary house, with a man working in the garden, whom we decided to sound out.

Leaving the other two hidden, Jak and I walked across and spoke to him. He was not particularly surprised to see British troops. Our Army had not as yet arrived, but apparently there were few German troops left in the area, and he began denouncing the Nazis pretty freely. He suggested that we walk for a quarter of a mile to the south, where he would meet us at the edge of the wood and provide us with a map. He was sorry he could not offer us any food, nor could he ask us into his house. The reason was that he had children, and they had been so indoctrinated by the Nazis that it would be impossible to trust them. They would certainly inform if any German troops happened to turn up. We had no alternative but to do as he proposed, but as we walked southwards, I sent Frank to double back and watch the man. He was to make sure that only the man left the house and that, when he did so, he followed the route he had given us, to go off in a different direction, there being no telephone wires to the house. To our relief, the German intended no treachery. Just about fifteen minutes later he returned with the map, followed by Frank.

As we stood at the edge of the wood looking southwards over the open fields towards the town of Hanover on that April evening, we heard the drone of approaching aircraft. Another air armada came in sight, consisting of hundreds of planes, which looked like American Mitchell bombers, flying in close formation. No German fighter planes intercepted them, and there was very little anti-aircraft fire. Straight to their target, the virtually defenceless town, sped the planes with their burden of death. Soon the drone of the air fleet was submerged by the rumblings of exploded bombs, until the ground beneath our feet was trembling with vibrations and we could hardly hear ourselves speak. The attack continued for several long minutes, then ceased abruptly. We could again hear the drone of the engines, now receding. Clouds of smoke and dust were erupting from what remained of the distant town.

The German had already placed his map on the grass and had started to explain the local geography, but during the assault he had stopped talking and watched the bombing with us.

"Poor devils," he remarked. "I wouldn't go anywhere near the town, if I were you. They'd kill you, as they've already killed other bomber pilots."

"Tell him not to worry about that," I said to Jak. "Tell him we don't want to go that way; we want to go westwards."

Jak explained that to the German.

"He says the road to the west is that little lane along the southern edge of the field," interpreted Jak. "The next village in that direction is about two miles away and is still occupied by German troops. The one beyond that is Ostenbostel, and he isn't sure whether the Germans are still there, but he's heard rumours that they've pulled out. There's a small prisoner-of-war camp nearby, and they wouldn't want to be anywhere near that when the village is captured. Three or four miles farther west still, there's another village," and he pointed it out on the map. "The Germans have definitely withdrawn from that one."

We spent some little time discussing our plan of action, making the German wait until we had reached a decision. Eventually we agreed that we must make for the third village, where we would definitely be safe from recapture. We would have to get a move on, for we wanted to find food and shelter before nightfall, and it would soon be dark. However, the state of euphoria induced by our success so far erased any feelings of hunger and fatigue. We bade the German a friendly farewell, thanked him and set off, using our map, in the direction which we hoped would lead us home.

After about an hour of heading towards the sinking sun, we came within sight of the first village, and I led on, frequently referring to the map in my hand. For the most part we kept in the shelter of woods, but sometimes we crept along under cover of hedges, and we had occasionally to make some detours. We passed about a mile north of the village, seeing no one and hoping that no one had seen us.

Once the houses of this village had faded into the back-ground, we veered south-westerly towards Ostenbostel. The countryside was still flat, but with plenty of woods and hedges. The grass was beginning to grow tall and was spangled with spring flowers. There was not a breath of wind, nor a cloud in the sky. It was a beautiful, tranquil spring evening, and the silence was so intense that we could almost hear the plants growing around us. Our progress was excellent, and we were feeling very pleased with ourselves — until we reached the river.

It was not a big river — only about thirty feet wide — but we were annoyed to find it there at all, as the map, by means of a thin blue line, had indicated only a minor stream. After wasting time looking for a bridge both north and south, we had no alternative but to plunge waist-deep into the chill water and wade across. On the far side we followed a hedge which led westward, one field's width from the road leading to

Ostenbostel, and by nightfall we reached the outskirts of the village.

We came to a house that seemed to be the residence of a small farmer. It was fairly isolated, about three or four hundred yards from its nearest neighbours. Creeping close in the dusk, I could see chinks of light from the edges of the black-out curtains. Evidently someone was at home. Still uncomfortably wet, as well as tired and hungry, we held a whispered council of war. Frank and Blackie (as we now called him) were in favour of sleeping in a wood for the night and then continuing to the "safe village" next morning. Jak and I wanted to knock at the door of the house and find out whether there were indeed German troops in Ostenbostel, since, if there were none, we might obtain food and shelter for the night.

Since we would be taking the main risk, our plan was accepted, and as we crept up to the back door, I briefed him regarding my plan. In the yard I picked up a piece of wood that looked like a pick-handle. With this raised high over my head, ready for immediate use, I stood in the shadow to the right of the door, covering Jak as he went forward to knock. He had to knock three or four times before we heard a shuffling of feet inside. The light was doused, and an old man, of about seventy, opened the door. I remained hidden while Jak addressed him.

"Where are the German soldiers in the village?"

The old man replied and Jak repeated in English: "He says they left this afternoon."

"Ask him if he's absolutely sure."

More conversation between Jak and the German.

"He's positive. He says he saw them go himself."

I stepped forward and pushed past the old man into the house, which we searched and found to be a small, two-bedroomed bungalow, so frequently associated with small-holdings. The only other occupant was an old lady, presumably his wife. I called over to Frank and Blackie, and when we were all inside, I instructed Jak.

"Tell the old man that we're from the *Luftlanda*," a word I'd picked up from the guard corporal a few days earlier and which I gathered was applied particularly to us Red Devils, "and that we have been landed, by parachute ahead of the tanks. Tell him that we're armed" — I patted my chest to indicate that I had a hidden gun "and that the tanks will be here tomorrow. Now he must take us at once to the burgomaster."

Whether the title of "burgomaster" was correct for the head man of the village I did not know, but the old fellow knew what I meant. He glanced again at us, four husky, unshaven, dirty Red Devils, and beckoned us to follow. He was shaking with fear.

We followed him into the village square, where he knocked at the door of a large house. Presently the door was opened by a large, fat German in his middle fifties, wearing a dressing-gown. It looked as though he had already settled down for the night. A brief conversation took place between him and the old man, who was holding his cap respectfully. Finally the burgomaster addressed us. He said he regretted that his English was very poor and asked if any of us spoke German. When

Jak confirmed that he knew enough for ordinary purposes, the burgomaster put on his official manner and said, "Who is your leader?" Jak nodded towards me. "Tell him that I am formally surrendering the village to him. Our own troops left earlier in the day."

Jak translated and I replied.

"Tell the burgomaster to get dressed and to inform everyone in the village that our tanks will be here tomorrow. Every house not showing a white flag will then be burnt to the ground. Tell him also that we don't want any trouble and we don't want to hurt anyone, but anyone who disobeys will be shot."

As I heard Jak getting near the end of the translation of this little speech, I put my hand inside my flying-smock, a gesture that was not lost on the burgomaster.

By this time several people had appeared in the square. The burgomaster passed them my instructions and then disappeared to get dressed. Soon the first bed-sheets appeared, hanging from upstairs windows. I was glad I had remembered about those white sheets, which I had first seen in Münster — ten days ago? — it seemed more like ten years. Anyhow, it looked as though my little bluff was working. I hoped I was not getting over-confident.

By the time the burgomaster reappeared, fully dressed, white flags were in evidence all around the square, and I had had time to formulate another set of instructions.

"'Tell him that our Intelligence Service has informed us that there is a prison camp in the village and he must take us there to release the prisoners. We will ensure that the prisoners do not harm the civilian population, provided everyone does as he is told. Tell him also that it is vital that everyone keeps calm until the tanks arrive. That way they should all survive."

When Jak had relayed these orders, the burgomaster led us to a large building at the corner of the square, where a yard had been enclosed by high chain-link fencing attached to concrete posts, with a barbed-wire barrier at the top. A key was produced, and the gates were about to be opened when the prisoners let out a chorus of delighted screams and I began to have second thoughts about releasing them at that hour.

There must have been about a hundred men and women inside the pen. They were mostly Poles, Russians and other East Europeans who had obviously been used as slave labour on the farms and factories in the neighbourhood, but we also found eight Canadian soldiers who had been captured soon after they had crossed the Rhine by boat and had been left behind by the retreating German army. Finding a platform for Jakoff, I dictated a speech which he relayed to the prisoners. I told them that, although they were now going to be released, they were advised to stay where they were for the night. The villagers would provide them with an evening meal, but there was to be no fighting or looting. To this the prisoners agreed. They had evidently not been very badly treated by the local people and were too delighted at obtaining their freedom to want to work off any grudges — for the present, at least.

I then opened the gates and, after inviting the Canadians to come outside, we four went in to make friends with the prisoners, who laughed, danced and embraced us. They offered us what scraps of food they had managed to hide and even invited us to enjoy their women for the night, an offer which we thought best to decline. After about half an hour of merry-making we felt confident that the prisoners would not get up to any mischief that night, so we left the pen, with the gates wide open, and walked back to the burgomaster's house with the eight Canadians.

The burgomaster's wife, a big, buxom, middle-aged *Hausfrau*, had prepared, no doubt with the help of neighbours, a meal of hot stew and large chunks of black bread for us and the Canadians which we wolfed down. It was our first substantial meal for four days, and we could not have enjoyed it more had it been a dinner at the Ritz.

It was now nearly midnight and the question of sleep came up. The Canadians offered to stand guard, four on and four off, for the whole night, while we slept. They said they had had nothing to do for the last few days except catch up on their sleep, and they were only too pleased to show their gratitude at being released. So it was arranged that Jak and I would sleep in the burgomaster's house, with Frank and Blackie next door, while the Canadians kept their eyes skinned for any trouble.

The burgomaster's wife treated us like sons. She had lost one on the Russian Front and was evidently relieved that at last the war seemed to be over for her.

She insisted on our discarding our wet clothes and ran us hot baths. After we had stripped completely naked, she came and took away our outer clothes for drying and our underclothes for washing. She looked at my socks, which were just about standing up on their own. "*Drei Woche*," I said, holding up three fingers to signify that it was three weeks since I had taken them off, or any of my other clothes for that matter. Naked as the day I was born, I climbed with Jak into a large double bed with crisp white sheets. Before we could even wish each other goodnight, darkness and oblivion closed down upon us.

We woke at about eight o'clock the next morning, to find the sun streaming in through the bedroom window and Mrs Burgomaster gently calling us. She had laid out ready all our clothing, clean and dry, together with soap, towels and razors, and said that breakfast would be ready as soon as we came downstairs. It took me several seconds to realize where I was. Then, jumping out of bed and looking out of the window, I could see a forest of white flags waving over the village centre. In about fifteen minutes, washed, shaven, dressed in clean, dry clothes and feeling a new man, I joined Jak, Frank and Blackie at the breakfast table. There we feasted on German sausage, black bread and ersatz coffee. It all tasted wonderful.

During breakfast we held a council of war. It seemed expedient to push on westwards, in case our bluff was called, but I was for trying to extract the maximum advantage from the situation. I told Jak to demand transport to take us to meet the advancing tanks. Here, however, we encountered a problem. There was no transport. The village had one or two old cars but no petrol. However, Frank, exploring the place after breakfast, found a horse and cart and promptly commandeered it. So, by about half-past-nine, we four were on the move again. We had to leave the Canadians behind, as there was not room in the cart for more than four, but we promised to send transport for them as soon as possible. We also went to see the prisoners again and advised them to stay where they were till the Army arrived.

The horse plodded slowly along in the bright April sunshine, and we sat enjoying life and feeling great. After an uneventful hour we came to the next village. This was the third on the list that our German informant had given us — the one which he was sure was cleared of German troops. And so it proved.

Halting in the middle of the village and using the cart as a platform, Jak needed no prompting from me on the procedure for taking control of a German village. He demanded of the small crowd that they send for the burgomaster — quick! A slightly uneasy pause ensued until that dignitary arrived. There was always the chance that one or two Nazi fanatics might put up a resistance, forcing us to reveal that we had no weapons. However, the villagers were evidently resigned to their fate. They knew that the Allied Armies could not be very far away and that their own defenders had abandoned them. No doubt it came as a shock that we had arrived from the east rather than the west, and they must have been further shaken by the apparition of four of the dreaded "*Luftlanda*" in their red berets, riding in a horse and cart, showing every intention of producing guns from inside their flying-smocks.

So no trouble occurred. Jak went through the same formalities as at Ostenbostel, and the burgomaster officially handed over the village to me. He then ran up and down the main street, shouting to the residents to put out their white flags or their houses would be burnt to the ground. We waited until we saw the order being obeyed. Then, having watered the horse and persuaded a local farmer to give him a nosebag of food, we continued on our way westwards.

By midday we found we were approaching yet another village and had already made up our minds to follow the same routine when, to our delight, we spotted a British jeep by the roadside. Sitting on a grassy bank was a section of commandos in their green berets, brewing up tea. They did not seem over-surprised to see us in our strange transport. All sorts of unusual things were happening in Germany at that time. I gave the sergeant in charge an account of what had happened during the past twenty-four hours and asked if he could arrange for the Canadians at Ostenbostel to be picked up. He immediately agreed and sent for another jeep. I climbed into it beside the driver, the sergeant followed with his driver, and off we went to consolidate our capture of the villages. I felt more like a Red Devil again, for the commandos had supplied us with arms.

Twenty minutes later we had picked up the Canadians and were on our return journey. We had just passed through the second village when, advancing up the road towards us, came a column of British tanks. Standing up in the jeep, I motioned to them to halt, and then I told their squadron commander about the two villages ahead. I explained how their burgomasters had surrendered, and I also informed him about the prisoners in the camp. It was, I thought, the least I could do, after the kind treatment we had received at Ostenbostel. Under the circumstances, I felt sure that the two burgomasters would have no regrets at having surrendered their villages to us. It was quite a remarkable coincidence that the tanks should turn up just at the time when I had told the Germans they would. The burgomasters would never realize how four unarmed Red Devils had bluffed them.

CHAPTER
TWENTY-TWO

Home Again

Returning to the commando post, I found Jak, Frank and Blackie already eating a lunch which I eyed with avidity. Three fried eggs each, with rashers of bacon, thick slices of fresh white bread smothered in butter, and mugs of steaming hot, sweet tea. The first real English meal any of us had had for three weeks. I could hardly wait for mine to be cooked. For the Canadians too it was a taste of paradise after prison fare. The commandos made us all very welcome, and we spent a pleasant hour sitting around and exchanging stories about our experiences.

It appeared that the commandos were now attached to our 6th Airborne Division. They had been advancing along the northern wing of the division's front, while D Company had been at the southern end. What was left of D Company was now reported to be ten or fifteen miles away to the south, and the sergeant offered to send us back there immediately after lunch. He had heard about the platoon being captured and was surprised, at this stage of the war, to find us still alive. He seemed to think that the odds had been heavily in favour of our being shot whilst prisoners.

While the Canadians and commandos were busy gossiping, Blackie called Jak, Frank and me to one side to discuss what we should do next.

"I don't know about you three," he said, "but, if it can be arranged, I'd rather not go back to what's left of D Company for a day or two. A few days at a rest centre would suit me fine. What do you say?"

We looked at each other and nodded. That was a programme to which we could subscribe.

"Now I don't want to pull rank," continued Blackie, "but I think it would be better if I took command of the party. Do you agree?"

Again we nodded. Now that we were back with the Army, it was obviously the proper thing to do. Indeed, there was no alternative.

"Right then, I'll see the commando CO, tell him we've had a rough time, exaggerate the hardships a bit and ask for transport back to Brigade HQ. The Canadians are going back there anyway, so there should be no problems. Then we can all have a few days' rest before rejoining D Company."

I smiled to myself and thought, even if old Blackie has not had much experience of soldiering in the field, he certainly seems to know how Army administration works.

Less than an hour later we drove away in a three-ton truck and, on reaching Brigade HQ in the late afternoon, were allocated billets and took it easy till supper-time. Then we bedded down for the night in a requisitioned house. This was more like it, we agreed. We had now slept in a bed for two nights running.

Next morning Blackie told us he had had an interview with the brigade major and had asked if we could be sent back to Divisional HQ for two or three days' rest since there did not seem to be the proper facilities at Brigade HQ. The request was promptly granted, so once again we all climbed aboard a three-ton truck.

At Divisional HQ it was chaos. Thousands of prisoners of war were being liberated daily, and we were completely engulfed by them. We said a brief farewell to Blackie, who was immediately submerged in the sea of soldiers, and we never saw him again.

Documentation had gone by the board. There was not even enough staff to attempt it. Sprinkled among the crowd were a fair number of red berets, most of them sitting on the heads of Red Devils of the 1st Airborne Division, who had been taken prisoner at Arnhem. The 6th Airborne Divisional HQ staff, who were doing their best to sort us out, naturally assumed that we three were from the 1st Airborne Division. Feeling no overpowering impulse to correct this illusion, we followed the crowd and found ourselves in a convoy heading for England.

Progress was leisurely. At the first night stop the men who needed kit, uniform and kitbags were issued with them. We did not need any kit, but we managed to obtain two kitbags each, which we soon filled. Most of the depots at which we halted *en route* seemed to be warehouses piled high with domestic and other goods, and before long our bags were bulging with rolls of curtain material, cigars and anything else we could lay hands on. We managed to stay together as a group and, while other men swopping yarns of their experiences, we pretended to be chatting amongst ourselves. We would have found it embarrassing to tell these men, many of whom had suffered hardships during four years or more of incarceration, that we had been prisoners for only four days and then not in a prison camp.

At every overnight stop we were on tenterhooks, wondering whether someone would ask for our credentials, but it was assumed that any necessary checking had already been done. We crossed the Rhine, where there were now two pontoon bridges, with a stream of trucks travelling in either direction. What a difference, I thought, from the last time I saw the Rhine, when from the porthole of the glider I had looked down on the smoke of battle below, while flak and tracer bullets were rocketing all around. Now everything appeared peaceful, though busy with the commerce of war.

We were living in comparative luxury. Every night we slept in a bed, and halts during the day were planned to coincide with mealtimes. As Brussels drew nearer, we thought, if only we can reach it, we may be able to wangle a few days' leave before we are sent back to D Company. That was the limit of our ambitions. We never dared to think of the chance that we might fly back to England.

But we were in luck. At Brussels Airport, where we were dropped, documentation was as lax as it had been along the route. One corporal did look suspiciously at the heavy kitbags we were lugging along, but everyone was too busy to pay as much attention. The planes were coming in and out on an endless shuttle service. As one plane landed, another came into view. As a plane was being loaded, more ex-prisoners were queuing up to get on the next. We joined a queue and presently were sitting on our kitbags in an old Dakota, on our way to an airfield in Essex.

There, for the first time since our homeward trip had started, documentation was serious. For one thing, Army pay books were required, so that we could be paid. We were also asked our rank and unit, but none of the checkers knew where our unit was supposed to be and, strangely enough, nobody asked how long we had been prisoners of war. Having gone through the processing mill, we were finally given army warrants for six weeks' prisoner-of-war leave. It seemed too good to be true! We had instructions to report back to camp 6½ weeks later, so we asked if we could all report to the same camp, which was immediately agreed.

Once again we climbed into an army truck and were taken to the nearest railway station, to catch the next train to London. We were still in a dream. We just could not believe our luck. Only ten days earlier we had been in action, and here we were, with six week's leave in recompense for our prisoner-of-war experiences — which had lasted just four days!

The excitement of getting back to England had pushed into the back of my mind thoughts of my comrades in the Red Devils. But the train journey gave me time to think, and I thought about D Company, those who were taken prisoner and those who were not, and hoped they had all survived. I felt guilty about ducking out of the war, but I am sure the colonel would have understood. We were always taught to use our initiative, and if Lady Luck was on your side, you should play to your good fortune.

Before arriving in London we exchanged addresses, declaring to each other that we would always keep in touch. When we had first been taken prisoner, less than two weeks earlier, Jak and Frank had been just two of the men in my section. I knew them quite well and was friendly with them, but not more so than with the others. Since then, though, we had been through so much together that we had become bosom pals. We had shared so many perils that we wanted to go on sharing, and for the first part of the leave we managed to spend quite a lot of time together. Then the inevitable loosening of ties began. Jak started courting strongly, and Frank found the journeys down from Cheshire becoming onerous. As for me, I landed a part-time job with my old firm, in order to have a bit of money in my pocket, for the six weeks' leave pay had dwindled alarmingly by the end of two weeks. A familiar pattern of events in Army life was being repeated. Groups of men are thrown together for a pupose and for a time become very close to each other. Once that purpose is accomplished, however, they tend to drift apart. I looked back over my Army career and remembered Frank Bailey and Tiger Charlesworth, then Tosser Barnes, and Joe French, and Bill Simpson. Until our capture

Tombstone Gibson had been my particular friend, and now, last of all, there were Jak and Frank. I knew all this, too, would not last — that soon I would be back on my own again.

Two or three weeks after my leave started, the war was officially declared over, and there were celebrations every night from VE-Day onwards. Life was very full. I had a part-time job, bringing in a good wage, and for the moment everyone wanted to know a soldier, especially one of those Red Devils who had done so much to help win the war. While the elation of victory was at its peak, my evenings were a succession of girls, dancing and drinking. Nobody would accept money for a drink, or a ride on a bus, or a seat in the pictures. It was marvellous while it lasted, but I knew that this, too, would not be for long.

The one thing that I found annoying during those weeks of leave was that everyone who spoke to me when I was wearing my Red Devil uniform asked me whether I had been at Arnhem. While I admired the feats of the 1st Airborne at Arnhem, that operation had been a failure, even though a glorious one. The career of the 6th, however, had been a catalogue of successes, culminating in the crossing of the Rhine and the advance into Germany. Like most of the other men of the 6th, I felt that the public was putting the emphasis in the wrong quarter.

When our leave came to an end, we reported back to a camp at High Wycombe. This was run by the General Services Corps, and ex-prisoners underwent the same sort of training that I had received during my first six weeks in the Army. There were medical examinations and physical and mental aptitude tests to see where we were best qualified to serve for the remainder of our time in the Army. The Army Demobilization Group numbers had now been published, and I learned that I had at least two more years before my release. Because I had volunteered to rejoin the Red Devils after my convalescence, and despite the shrapnel still in my leg, I was worried that I might be graded A1. That could mean transfer to the Far East, where the war against Japan still looked a very long way from being over. It was a prospect which I viewed with apprehension. Nevertheless, I was pleased to be with Jak and Frank again, and life at the camp was easy, compared to what we were used to in the Army.

Eventually our postings came through. Jak was to join an infantry regiment in the north of England. Frank and I had been recommended to attend an officers' training course, with a view to signing on for short-service commissions. Frank accepted. He became a second lieutenant with an infantry regiment in Trieste and finished up with the rank of captain. I refused, for the second time in my Army career. Every officer I had respected as a leader had, with the exception of Lieutenant Weeks, been killed or wounded. The fatality risk was too high. On the other hand, as an officer I would certainly not want to be like Percy Pearman or Captain O'Neil. I would like to inspire my men and lead them into action. Then I would probably be killed, and I did not want that. So I declined.

Fortunately, the interviewing officer was very understanding. He seemed to be considerably impressed by my war record.

"I think you've done your share," he told me, "even though you were only out of the country for a total of three months. You seem to have been in continuous action and danger for all that time. I notice that you've had shorthand training, so I'm recommending that you finish the rest of your Army service at the War Office, billeted at home."

"Thank you very much, sir," I said and saluted.

After a course to sharpen up my shorthand, I finished my Army career as a sergeant shorthand writer on Field Marshal Montgomery's staff at the War Office.

Jak was as disappointed with his posting as Frank and I were pleased with ours. We were due for one more weekend together before we separated, and Frank and I spent it as guests of his sister at her flat in Chelsea. Jak meantime went off to see his girl-friend and it was no surprise on the Sunday night to find that he was not on the train. He had gone Absent Without Leave. I never saw him again, nor, I suspect, did the Army.

Neither was it surprising on Monday morning, immediately after breakfast, to hear over the tannoy that I was wanted at the CO's office.

"I'll bet it's to do with that bloody fool Jak," I exclaimed to Frank as I dashed off to report to the sergeant-major.

It was the usual performance — left-right, left-right, halt, right turn. I saluted the CO.

"At ease, Corporal," the CO smiled. "I've got a rather special task for you."

"Very good, sir," I said, respectfully.

"As you are aware, you and your two colleagues are the only airborne men on the camp. I would like you to take one of them along with you to represent the camp at a garden party at Buckingham Palace that the King and the royal family are giving to ex-prisoners of war. Would you like to do that for me?"

"Very much, sir," I replied. "And I'd like to take Private Ponsonby with me."

"Very well," said the major. "The garden party is tomorrow, and I understand you are being posted on Wednesday, so if you and Ponsonby would like to take your kit and draw your travel warrants, you may have the rest of the day off. Go home if you like, attend the garden party and then on to your new posting Wednesday morning."

"Thank you very much, sir."

"Now here are the tickets for the Palace. You have to assemble at Chelsea Barracks at noon tomorrow. Then the column will march to the Palace, and it could be all over by four o'clock. Any more questions?"

"No, sir; and thank you, sir. We'll be looking our best, sir."

I saluted, left the office and ran back to the hut to find Frank as quickly as I could. Together we packed our gear and drew our travel warrants and posting instructions. We were out of the camp within half an hour, before anyone had noticed that Jakoff was missing and could start to ask us questions about him.

Tuesday dawned a sunny day. Hundreds of troops of all ranks and regiments, from colonels to privates and from guardsmen to Pioneer Corps, gathered in Chelsea Barracks. With bands playing, our column set out to march to Bucking-ham Palace. In through the gates we went, through the archway and into a large courtyard in the centre of the Palace. There, breaking step, we walked through stately rooms that reminded me of a museum, and so on to the lawns.

The column re-formed while the King, the Queen and the two princesses walked slowly along the ranks, talking to some of us. The King actually stopped and had a word with me, asking how I was after my prisoner-of-war experiences.

"Very well, Your Majesty," I nervously replied.

Then the parade broke up, and the royal party mingled casually with the crowd, chatting to small groups. However, Frank and I had noticed the delicacies laid out on tables in an immense, open-fronted marquee. They seemed more exciting to two twenty-year-olds than even a chat with royalty.

When the royal party had retired into the Palace, we drifted slowly to the gates, where Frank and I were to part, and I wished him all the best in his new career.

"All the best to you too, Andy," replied Frank, "though with your home posting you should have it nice and easy."

"I hope so," said I. "I can do without any more action."

"Me too," he replied, "but I felt I had to try for a commission, even if it means I shall be in the Army a year longer than you. You've seen more fighting than I have, and you have led troops into action, which is something I haven't yet done, though I don't know that I much look forward to it. Tell me, Andy, looking back over all your Army experiences, when were you most afraid?"

I did not hesitate.

"Seeing those men in there, most of whom had been prisoners of war for so many long years," I said. "I was dead scared the King was going to ask me how long I'd been prisoner of war."

ISIS publish a wide range of books in large print, from fiction to biography. Any suggestions for books you would like to see in large print or audio are always welcome. Please send to the Editorial department at:

ISIS Publishing Ltd.
7 Centremead
Osney Mead
Oxford OX2 0ES
(01865) 250 333

A full list of titles is available free of charge from:
Ulverscroft large print books

(UK)
The Green
Bradgate Road, Anstey
Leicester LE7 7FU
Tel: (0116) 236 4325

(Australia)
P.O Box 953
Crows Nest
NSW 1585
Tel: (02) 9436 2622

(USA)
1881 Ridge Road
P.O Box 1230, West Seneca,
N.Y. 14224-1230
Tel: (716) 674 4270

(Canada)
P.O Box 80038
Burlington
Ontario L7L 6B1
Tel: (905) 637 8734

(New Zealand)
P.O Box 456
Feilding
Tel: (06) 323 6828

Details of **ISIS** complete and unabridged audio books are also available from these offices. Alternatively, contact your local library for details of their collection of **ISIS** large print and unabridged audio books.